THE HOUSE
OF HIS
CHOOSING...

A Solid Foundation for the 21st Century Church

Pastor Doug

I trust this will be
a blessing to you.
thanks for your help.

Jim West

THE HOUSE
OF HIS
CHOOSING...

A Solid Foundation for the 21st Century Church

JIM WIES

Destiny Image® Publishers, Inc.
P.O. Box 310
Shippensburg, PA 17257-0310

"Speaking to the Purposes of God for This Generation
and for the Generations to Come"

ISBN 0-7684-2041-5

For Worldwide Distribution
Printed in the U.S.A.

This book and all other Destiny Image, Revival Press,
and Treasure House books are available
at Christian bookstores and distributors worldwide.

For a U.S. bookstore nearest you, call **1-800-722-6774**.
For more information on foreign distributors, call **717-532-3040**.
Or reach us on the Internet: **http://www.reapernet.com**

Acknowledgments

There is a group of people I would like to give my thanks and acknowledgment to—the wonderful congregation of Cornerstone Church of DeFuniak Springs, Florida. It has been a grand and awesome stewardship from God to be able to live among and give leadership to such a loving family of believers for the last ten years. I want to thank this gracious and loving "family" for their love of God, love of one another, and their love for me and my family.

A hearty thanks as well for their patience with a pastor who could, more often than not, be found "holed up" in his office studying and thinking; or at times have to be called "back to earth" from the "heights of thought and meditation" he so often drifted to, during the times of the early formation of the content of this book. I truly consider it one of the highlights of my life to have spent these last ten years leading this church. Thank you!

There is one other person certainly worthy of my mention: my pastor, mentor, employer, and friend for the previous ten years, Pastor Ron Woodworth. Thanks for introducing me to the idea that there are apostles and prophets in the church today, and believing in me when I didn't look like one.

Endorsements

The House of His Choosing... is refreshingly focused on Jesus the "Cornerstone" of the building, while bringing to our attention the vital and foundational ministries of prophets and apostles. This book contains insights into how and why apostles and prophets must co-labor together to lay the proper foundations for effective churches.

Jim's book has revelatory insight into God's intentions for the church at the end of the age, and at the same time has functional wisdom gained from practical experience. Although leaders will enjoy it for the solid restorational truths contained in it, followers of Jesus will be strengthened in their knowledge and insight into the Lord and their place in God's overall end-time purposes for the church.

Mike Bickle
Internationally known conference speaker
Pastor of Metro Christian Fellowship
Kansas City, Missouri
Author of: *Passion for Jesus*
Growing in the Prophetic

Jim Wies has been a consistent student of the foundational ministries of apostle and prophet. He has himself demonstrated the unique ability to function as a prophetic voice in the disciplines of a pastoral role. His new book looks first at the author of the fivefold, Jesus Himself. It then unfolds this expression of Jesus in the church. Jim's perspective is a "safe haven" for pastors and leaders who have feared the emerging of these vital gifts. He and his wife, Carolyn, have been trusted friends, confidants, and prophetic voices into the churches I have served. Read, absorb, and grow!

Steve Witt
Church planter and apostolic team member with
"Partners In Harvest, International"
Pastor of Metro Church South
Cleveland, Ohio

Written from a prophetic perspective, *The House of His Choosing...* captures the fundamental essence of God's present work of restoration in the church on earth today. Beginning from a specific focus on the person and work of the Lord Jesus, Jim presents a compelling argument for the church as an interdependent reality. However, this text takes one beyond the nearly passé treatment of the necessity of Ephesians 4:11 teamwork. Here we are presented with precise issues that must be addressed if we are to build the church with integrity, balance, and authentic spiritual power. As such, *The House of His Choosing...* is an excellent introduction to prophetic revelation, which according to Proverbs 29:18, is the linchpin of effective spiritual leadership.

Worthy of note is that the author is far more than a mere theoretician. As an effective local pastor, faithful husband and father, and proven prophetic voice, Jim Wies is speaking from experience borne by God's refining fires. For nearly 25 years now, I have observed Jim's emergence into recognized public ministry. Always faithful, always loyal, and always passionate about serving Christ, I can attest to the authenticity of Jim's character and message. It is without reservation, therefore, that I wholeheartedly endorse Jim's work as deserving studied attention from those who are truly seeking to know what the Spirit is saying to the church.

Ron Woodworth
Pastor of Lord of Life Church
Phoenix, Arizona

Jim Wies is a soul winner, a biblical expositor, my pastor, my mentor, and my friend. Every page of *The House of His Choosing...* is supported biblically. This is sound doctrine based on God's written Word. This is a big little book!

From "A View From Above the Knothole" to the use of the personalities of Jonah and Jeremiah to illustrate relationship blockage, this book makes you think, not in the concentric circles of systematic theology, but in the "big picture," that is, "What is God doing now, and how?"

Some say a book is worth its price if you gain one ministry principle from it; if so, the last chapter alone is reason enough to buy this one.

As a teacher, Jim Wies consistently presents principles that are tied directly to Scripture. This book follows that pattern, revealing what God is doing in His end-time church. If you believe in finding where God is working and joining Him there, read this book!

Read with a Bible in one hand and this book in the other. See clearly what God is up to in these last days!

G. Barrett Glover
Senior Chaplain
Washington Correctional Institute, Florida

The body of Christ has been undergoing a radical change to a degree not experienced since the days of Martin Luther. I call it the New Apostolic Reformation. Jim Wies sees and understands this important movement very well. As he analyzes it in this book, he brings fresh biblical and practical clarity to many crucial issues, healthy insights that cannot be found elsewhere. *The House of His Choosing...* will help you hear accurately what the Spirit is saying to the churches.

C. Peter Wagner
Wagner Leadership Institute

When the two key elements of devotion and godly government unite, we find an increase in the heat of God's purifying fire. Hope dawns, lives are changed, the "house" is repaired. It happened in Hezekiah's day, under Josiah's reign, and was perfectly displayed through Jesus.

The Father continues to search for leaders who will catch His dream and build with the imperishable materials of the Spirit rather than the resources of this world, such as ambition, pride, control, etc. He is looking for leaders who will say, "The zeal of Your house has consumed me." Jim's book offers encouraging insight into God's pattern for His "house" as we co-labor with Jesus in these glorious days of renewal and restoration.

Beverly Spaulding
Musician/Prophetic Psalmist
Author of: *The Way of Holiness*
And Looking We Are Changed
The Ministry of the Psalmist
The Shepherd and the Bride

Jim Wies is a man of great integrity and character. His revelation and understanding of the church and what God is doing today is birthed from the Spirit of God. I consider Jim and his wife, Carolyn, to be friends, and I want to personally commend and recommend his new book, *The House of His Choosing...* to all who are looking to grow in the wisdom and knowledge of God and end-time ministry.

Ron Cohen
Messianic Miracle Ministries

Jim Wies has written one of the most invigorating books on the church I've ever experienced. Surely Pastor Wies has been before God to get such insight, because only the Spirit of God could have revealed to him the order, purpose, and function of the church with such clarity. This book will be a significant assistance to us as leaders to equip the saints to lead those who are lost to the salvation of our Lord Jesus Christ.

Willie Blackmon
Church planter
Pastor of Gospel of the Kingdom of Heaven Church
DeFuniak Springs, Florida

Contents

Foreword

Pastor Jim Wies has given an outstanding presentation of Christ's glorious house, His church.

Jesus Christ is shown as the true example and living demonstration of all fivefold ministers of apostle, prophet, evangelist, pastor, and teacher. He rightly reveals that Christ Jesus is to be the center of all Christian ministers and ministries.

Jim brings forth fresh revelation truth concerning the foundational ministries of apostle and prophet. The church is shown to be like a house with divine structure and government with every member being a vital part of the complete building that is being built together for an habitation of God through the Spirit.

Pastors will especially appreciate the sound wisdom and proper protocol for the function of prophets and prophetic ministry within the local church.

Pastor Wies has more than a decade of experience in pastoring a prophetic church. He also has functioned personally as a prophet while ministering in other churches and conferences in different parts of the world. Pastor Jim has had many prophets minister in his local church, which has given him much experience in dealing with prophetic utterances and supernatural manifestations of the Holy Spirit.

Jim exemplifies the heart of God when he talks of God's desire for unity in His church. He reveals through biblical truths and examples that the last-day fivefold ministers will not be "lone rangers" but team players who have authority because they are under authority with proper relationship to each other. They are completely committed to Christ and His cause. They are more interested in promoting the greater good and the overall purpose of Christ and His church than promoting their own ministry.

This book contains a wealth of wisdom and practical truths. All who read it will grow in the graces and knowledge of Jesus Christ while being established in present truth. God bless you, Jim, for loving Christ enough to take the time and effort to make these wonderful truths available to the body of Christ.

Dr. Bill Hamon
Bishop of Christian International Ministries Network
Author of: *Prophets and Personal Prophecy*
Prophets and the Prophetic Movement
Prophets, Pitfalls and Principles
Apostles, Prophets and the Coming Moves of God
Fulfilling Your Personal Prophecy
Prophetic Destiny and the Apostolic Reformation

Introduction

A View From Above the Knothole

The story is told about a young boy who had never seen a baseball game before. He was curious about a local game, but he didn't have money for a ticket. Around one side of the stadium was a high wooden fence, and to his delight, the boy discovered a knothole in the fence. He peeked through to see what the game was all about.

After he watched for awhile, he became a bit disillusioned by what he saw. There were two men standing in a field who would occasionally move forward and then back. Then they would run off to an area that he couldn't see and two new men would come out. And there were bleachers full of people watching them do this. He was beginning to think that baseball wasn't such a great sport until a buddy came along and together they climbed up a nearby tree. The view from high in the tree branches was quite different than the one he had seen by looking through the knothole. Now he saw all the action. He realized that he had been viewing only a very limited part of the game. He realized that things look quite different from above the knothole.

We, as Christians, have often been in the same position with our faith as the boy who was looking through the knothole. We have a limited view of God and His church. For centuries, we viewed the church from the limited perspective of our own experiences and the traditions of men. With such a narrow perspective, it is no wonder that most people think there has to be something more to Christianity than we are currently seeing—and there is. But to get the proper view, we must step back, rise above the knothole, and see the bigger perspective.

This book is an attempt to gain a fresh perspective by rising above what we have seen of the church so far and taking a look at what it could be and will be. God is planning a glorious end-time expression of the church full of apostolic power, prophetic revelation, and unprecedented love of the brethren—a church that is one even as the Father and the Son are one, giving proof to the world that Jesus is from the Father (see Jn. 17). This stretches our faith, but I believe that since Jesus prayed it, it will happen. God promised David that He would raise up the house of David and a descendant of David would rule there forever.

> *And with this the words of the prophets agree, just as it is written: "After this I will return and will rebuild the tabernacle of David, which has fallen down; I will rebuild its ruins, and I will set it up; so that the rest of mankind may seek the Lord, even all the Gentiles who are called by My name, says the Lord who does all these things." Known to God from eternity are all His works* (Acts 15:15-18).

This tabernacle, the "house of David," is the church that Jesus Christ, the Son of David, said that He would build and that even the gates of hell would not be able to prevail against (see Mt. 16:18).

We are at a place of major transition and restoration in the church. Acts 3:20-21 (NAS) states that Jesus is being retained in the heavens "...until the period of restoration of all things about which God spoke by the mouth of His holy prophets from ancient time." We are in the final stages of that period. But in order to see the final version of the church in all its restoration glory, we must also see the church's apostolic and prophetic foundations restored. A church with a fully restored and functioning fivefold ministry will be a whole new ball game. The end-time vision of the church is directly connected to the restoration of end-time apostles and prophets.

I am pleased to add this book to a growing body of material bringing clarity to the vital and foundational ministries of apostles and prophets, whose primary task is to reveal the person of Jesus Christ and the resultant spiritual "house" that God declared that He would build from the beginning. It is my prayer that this book will grant to us a fresh perspective of the church as we attempt to see the bigger picture from "above the knothole."

Section I

The Cornerstone Revealed

So this is what the Sovereign Lord says: "See, I lay a stone in Zion, a tested stone, a precious cornerstone for a sure foundation; the one who trusts will never be dismayed" (Isaiah 28:16 NIV).

Chapter 1

Fixing Our Eyes on Jesus— The Mystery of Ages

Paul the apostle spoke of a mystery that was at last being revealed by God to all of creation, including the principalities and powers in the heavenlies. In Ephesians 3:5 he speaks of this mystery "which in other ages was not made known to the sons of men, as it has now been revealed by the Spirit to His holy apostles and prophets." So what is this mystery that is uniquely being revealed in this day? The Scriptures go on to say that the mystery pertains to this glorious entity called the church, comprised of what was once irreconcilable parts, but which are now reconciled and made into one body in Christ.

Paul felt humbled that God would entrust to him this stewardship— the unfolding of the unsearchable riches of Christ; the revelation of the church; and the revelation that the church has been given stewardship of "...the administration of the mystery which for ages has been hidden in God...." The purpose was "that the manifold wisdom of God might now be made known through the church to the rulers and the authorities in the heavenly places" (Eph. 3:9-10 NAS).

The church seems to have a unique place, and apostles and prophets in particular, in the administration of this mystery. Although there are many other aspects to the work of apostles and prophets and to the foundational place they have in the church, one function is primary. That is the ability to unfold the revelation of the unified corporate body called "the church," revealing who Jesus is to mankind and to all creation.

The greatest purpose apostolic and prophetic ministries have, their ultimate goal above all else, is to offer a revelation of Jesus, to show forth the light of the unfolding of the unsearchable riches found in Jesus. They are to reveal the Cornerstone, who is Christ Jesus Himself! What better place then to begin a book about apostles and prophets than to bring light upon who Jesus is?

Seeing Jesus in Our Mountaintop Experiences

Jesus promised His disciples that some of them would not taste death before they would actually see the Son of Man revealed in the glory of His Father. It was just six days later when Jesus called Peter, James, and John aside and led them to a mountain. You might say that they were in for a real "mountaintop" experience. The story is told in Matthew 17:1-8:

> *Now after six days Jesus took Peter, James, and John his brother, led them up on a high mountain by themselves; and He was transfigured before them. His face shone like the sun, and His clothes became as white as the light. And behold, Moses and Elijah appeared to them, talking with Him. Then Peter answered and said to Jesus, "Lord, it is good for us to be here; if You wish, let us make here three tabernacles: one for You, one for Moses, and one for Elijah." While he was still speaking, behold, a bright cloud overshadowed them; and suddenly a voice came out of the cloud, saying, "This is My beloved Son, in whom I am well pleased. Hear Him!" And when the disciples heard it, they fell on their faces and were greatly afraid. But Jesus came and touched them and said, "Arise, and do not be afraid." When they had lifted up their eyes, they saw no one but Jesus only.*

We are quick to laugh at Peter's bumbling attempt to respond to the incredible sight that was occurring before him, yet how many can honestly say that we haven't been guilty of the same thing? How many of us have reveled in our own mountaintop experiences in God and become enamored with the experience rather than enamored with the God who brought us the experience? There are many things coming to light in these days of restoration that are spectacular in themselves. I must admit that at times I have been quite infatuated with the things of His Kingdom, such as the prayer movement that is sweeping the earth, the resurgence of power gifts and miracles in our day, or the prophetic and apostolic movements...the list could go on and on. Yet it is a mistake to fix our eyes on anything less than Jesus Himself. Although movements are valuable of themselves and are given by God to advance His purposes, any time we get our eyes onto the event and off the Lord, we have missed His primary purpose for it.

Moses and Elijah appeared with Jesus. There was nothing wrong with Moses, and there was nothing wrong with Elijah. In fact, their appearance was a glorious miracle. They spoke significant things about who Jesus actually was. Elijah's appearance was a powerful prophetic fulfillment of Old Testament Scriptures concerning the coming of Messiah. Yet in the light of the glorified Jesus, their significance faded. In this setting God spoke out of a cloud, telling the disciples to keep their focus on Jesus.

This story still speaks to us today. In this incident, Moses stands as a type of apostolic ministry and Elijah of prophetic ministry. God is bringing to light many truths about the fully restored ministry of apostles and prophets in this day. As He does this, we will see Jesus glorified before all mankind.

As long as the disciples had their focus on men, even these great men, they stood upright and presumptuous. It was when they saw the revelation of the glorious Christ, which the Father was showing them, that they fell in humility before God who alone shall be glorified when all is said and done. Though the emergence of apostles and prophets is exciting and intriguing, we will do well to hear the Father's words echoing down through the centuries to us: "This is My Son...I'm pleased with Him...Listen to what He has to say." We must keep our eyes fixed on Jesus.

"Sir, We Wish to See Jesus!"

One of the most intriguing stories we see in Scripture occurred as Jesus' fame was spreading abroad toward the end of His earthly ministry and is told in the Gospel of John chapter 12. It happened following one of the most spectacular events of His ministry, the raising of Lazarus from the dead. Jesus had become the talk of the town.

The Pharisees were out to kill Him, but the crowds were clamoring to see Him. As is human nature, all the curiosity seekers came to check things out. Some were there because they wanted to "see that guy who was raised from the dead." Others undoubtedly just wanted to be where the crowd was. It was during that time when the feast of Passover was approaching. Jesus had returned to Lazarus' home, just outside of Jerusalem. The story picks up in John 12:9:

> *Now a great many of the Jews knew that He was there; and they came, not for Jesus' sake only, but that they might also see Lazarus, whom He had raised from the dead.*

Such is also the condition of the church today. There are many who rush to see for themselves the latest phenomena instead of seeking the Lord who originated the phenomena. This passage of Scripture goes on to describe the great processional in which Jesus came riding into Jerusalem on a colt while children prophetically declared, "Hosanna! 'Blessed is He who comes in the name of the Lord!' The King of Israel!" (Jn. 12:13) We will discuss this event in more detail later in the book, but right now, I want to focus on one certain group of hungry seekers who expressed the same yearning that many of us have today.

In the midst of the crowd we find a band of seekers who were looking past the party, past the "Lazarus phenomena," and past the traditions of the moment.

> *Now there were certain Greeks among those who came up to worship at the feast. Then they came to Philip, who was from Bethsaida of Galilee, and asked him, saying, "Sir, we wish to see Jesus." Philip came and told Andrew, and in turn Andrew and Philip told Jesus. But Jesus answered them, saying, "The hour has come that the Son of Man should be glorified"* (John 12:20-23).

Their request was, "Sir, we wish to see Jesus." This is the cry resonating in the heart of many genuine seekers, and it is this request that last-day leaders must recognize as the one request we must answer. We must lead people to Jesus. Our goal must be to glorify Jesus and point the serious seekers to Him. The heart cry of a seeking humanity is "Take me past the programs, take me past the fad of the moment, take me past the apostles, the signs and wonders, the crowds, and the processional. Sir, we wish to see Jesus!"

Although this book is dedicated to the purpose of unfolding important truths about the church, the emerging apostolic movement, and the various aspects of team ministry within the fivefold leadership, we must always hold these things in proper perspective to the primary objective— to reveal Jesus. It is Jesus that men need to see. There is the cry in the heart of the people of God to the leaders of the church today saying, "Sir, we wish to see Jesus. We've had enough of lesser things; we want to see Jesus." And just as Andrew and Philip of old, we must point them to Jesus.

Signs and Wonders—Pointing to Jesus

We must reveal Jesus. People want to see Jesus, not our finely honed theological statements. People want to see Jesus, not our fine worship bands. People want to see Jesus, not our latest sign phenomenon.

Yes, the phenomenon will draw a crowd for a little while, but then are we, like these two faithful apostles, pointing them to Jesus?

Whenever there is a new round of signs and wonders in the church, a polarization within the body of Christ arises almost as quickly about whether these signs and wonders were divine or counterfeit. The fact is that in any given case, it could be either. How would you answer this question? Someone turns a rod into a serpent: Is it a divine sign and wonder or a counterfeit? Well, in Scripture, we see that it could be either, as in the case of Moses and the Egyptian magicians.

A sign is an abnormal, unusual "attention getter" designed to point to something. Here, where I live in Northwest Florida, there are lots and lots of trees. In fact, I live in the midst of miles and miles of pine forests. If I were to tell someone to drive down the road for a few miles until they saw the pine tree on the left and turn there, they would most certainly become lost since there are hundreds of trees that all look pretty much the same. If, on the other hand, I said, "Look for the pine tree that has been sawed into planks, nailed together, painted white and has an arrow on it pointing left" (i.e., a sign), it would be much easier to find the destination that sign pointed to.

The fact is that a sign is simply an unusual "something" that gets our attention. A sign is of necessity an unusual, abnormal phenomenon. Otherwise, it would not serve its purpose. The validity of the sign is found not in what the sign is but in what the sign points to. The sign phenomenon itself cannot be the sole criteria by which we judge whether it is divine or counterfeit. A sign is meant to point to something. What it points to makes all the difference.

This leads us to another principle. The sign is not the destination, but it points us to the destination. In all cases, our destination should be Jesus. That is the criteria by which to judge signs and wonders.

> *If there arises among you a prophet or a dreamer of dreams, and he gives you a sign or a wonder, and the sign or the wonder comes to pass, of which he spoke to you, saying, "Let us go after other gods"—which you have not known—"and let us serve them," you shall not listen to the words of that prophet or that dreamer of dreams, for the Lord your God is testing you to know whether you love the Lord your God with all your heart and with all your soul* (Deuteronomy 13:1-3).

The accuracy of a word, the validity of a sign, or the value of anything else is not measured by whether it is an authentic miracle, but whether it glorifies Jesus. Can God give golden fillings to people's teeth?

Absolutely. Can the enemy counterfeit it? Quite probably. The true question is, in the meetings in which this occurs, is the name of Jesus being lifted up? Is the gospel being preached? Are people being provoked to deeper devotion to Jesus? Are they recovering their first love for the Lord? These are the real criteria. I would venture to say that from group to group those criteria may differ. Let's not judge a group or event by the phenomenon of itself but by the criteria of what the signs and wonders are pointing to.

People need to see Jesus, the living Word, who was in the beginning, who was with God, and who is God. People need to be pointed to Jesus, who left the glory of Heaven, was born of a virgin, took upon Himself the form of a man, and as a man faced every temptation and trial that we will ever face, and did so without sinning once.

People need to see Jesus, who said, "Most assuredly, I say to you, unless one is born again, he cannot see the kingdom of God" (Jn. 3:3b). People need to be pointed to Jesus, of whom it was said: "For God so loved the world that He gave His only begotten Son, that whoever believes in Him should not perish but have everlasting life" (Jn. 3:16).

People need to see Jesus, who said, "I am the bread of life. He who comes to Me shall never hunger, and he who believes in Me shall never thirst" (Jn. 6:35). They need the One who said, "I am the light of the world. He who follows Me shall not walk in darkness, but have the light of life" (Jn. 8:12b). They need the One who said, "Most assuredly, I say to you, before Abraham was, I AM" (Jn. 8:58b) and, "I am the door. If anyone enters by Me, he will be saved" (Jn. 10:9a).

People need to see Jesus, who said, "I am the good shepherd. The good shepherd gives His life for the sheep" (Jn. 10:11). They need to see Jesus who said, "I am the resurrection and the life. He who believes in Me, though he may die, he shall live" (Jn. 11:25).

People need to see Jesus, who said, "I am the way, the truth, and the life. No one comes to the Father except through Me" (Jn. 14:6). They need to see Jesus, who said, "I am the vine, you are the branches. He who abides in Me, and I in him, bears much fruit; for without Me you can do nothing" (Jn. 15:5).

People want to see Jesus by whose wounds we are healed, for it was He who bore our sins in His body on the cross and whose blood cleanses us of all our sin. He died, was buried, and rose again on the third day with victory over sin and death (see Is. 53; Heb. 9:22; 10:19; 1 Pet. 2:24; 1 Jn. 1:7; Rev. 1:5).

People are yearning to see this same Jesus, who was seen by over 500 people after His resurrection, who ascended back through the clouds to take His seat at the right hand of the Majesty in Heaven, and who is seated in the heavenly realms making intercession for us (see Acts 1:11; 1 Cor. 15:6; Heb. 7:25).

People need to be pointed to Jesus, who has been exalted far above all rule and authority, power and dominion, and every title that can be given, not only in the present age but also in the one to come (see Phil. 2:9-11). They need to know the One before whom every knee shall bow in heaven and on earth and under the earth and whom every tongue will acknowledge as Lord.

People need to see Jesus, who is Himself the King of kings and Lord of lords. They need to be pointed to Jesus, of whom ten thousand times ten thousand, and thousands of thousands say in heaven, "Worthy is the Lamb who was slain to receive power and riches and wisdom, and strength and honor and glory and blessing" (Rev. 5:12). If we see Him properly, we will understand that He is the solution to our every problem. He is the answer to mankind's searching. We need to see Jesus as the proper goal of all our searching. The Greek foreigners in our passage above were looking in the right direction.

We need to see Jesus, the Cornerstone, the frame of reference for all that is built and anything that is done of eternal value, for from Him and to Him and through Him are all things (see Col. 1:15-20). To Him be the glory, forever and ever, amen.

Seeing Jesus—God's Gift to Man

Thanks be to God for His indescribable gift! (2 Corinthians 9:15)

I am regularly stimulated to new dimensions of interest in my pursuit of the knowledge of God when I see statements such as Paul made referring to Jesus as an "indescribable gift" or when he mentions "the unsearchable riches of Christ" or states that we may "know the love of Christ which passes knowledge" (see Eph. 3:17-19). How do we begin to describe an "indescribable gift," plumb the depths of "unsearchable riches," or know that which "passes knowledge"? I would dare to state that few have had a deeper knowledge and revelation of Christ Jesus than Paul the apostle, yet look at his amazing statement in his letter to the Philippians:

More than that, I count all things to be loss in view of the surpassing value of knowing Christ Jesus my Lord, for whom I have suffered the loss of all things, and count them but rubbish in order that I may gain Christ, and may be found in Him, not having a righteousness of my own derived from the Law, but that which is through faith in Christ, the righteousness which comes from God on the basis of faith, that I may know Him, and the power of His resurrection and the fellowship of His sufferings, being conformed to His death; in order that I may attain to the resurrection from the dead (Philippians 3:8-11 NAS).

Paul valued the knowledge of God above any earthly thing. He gave it all away for what he called the surpassing value of knowing Christ.

So what is this "indescribable gift" that is so comprehensive that the deepest theologians can plumb its depths for centuries without ever fully comprehending all its implications, yet is so simple that a child can comprehend and receive this gift by faith for the saving of their soul? It is, of course, none other than the Father's gift of His Son Jesus Christ.

For God so loved the world that He gave His only begotten Son, that whoever believes in Him should not perish but have everlasting life (John 3:16).

Paul very succinctly summarized the gospel this way in his letter to the Corinthians:

Moreover, brethren, I declare to you the gospel which I preached to you, which also you received and in which you stand, by which also you are saved, if you hold fast that word which I preached to you— unless you believed in vain. For I delivered to you first of all that which I also received: that Christ died for our sins according to the Scriptures, and that He was buried, and that He rose again the third day according to the Scriptures, and that He was seen by Cephas, then by the twelve. After that He was seen by over five hundred brethren at once, of whom the greater part remain to the present, but some have fallen asleep. After that He was seen by James, then by all the apostles. Then last of all He was seen by me also, as by one born out of due time. ... Therefore, whether it was I or they, so we preach and so you believed (1 Corinthians 15:1-8,11).

His body was broken and His blood was shed for us. Then He rose from the dead, giving proof that the work was thorough and sufficient. Through that one dramatic act of selfless giving comes to us all the grace, mercy, provision, and salvation we need. All Heaven's bounty is now available through and only through the cross of Christ Jesus.

He is the source of your life in Christ Jesus, whom God made our wisdom, our righteousness and sanctification and redemption; therefore, as it is written, "Let him who boasts, boast of the Lord" (1 Corinthians 1:30-31 RSV).

He was in the world, and the world was made through Him, and the world did not know Him. He came to His own, and His own did not receive Him. But as many as received Him, to them He gave the right to become children of God, to those who believe in His name: who were born, not of blood, nor of the will of the flesh, nor of the will of man, but of God. ...and we beheld His glory, the glory as of the only begotten of the Father, full of grace and truth. ... For the law was given through Moses, but grace and truth came through Jesus Christ (John 1:10-14,17).

Look at the implications of this gift from God as written in the Epistle to the Romans.

What then shall we say to these things? If God is for us, who can be against us? He who did not spare His own Son, but delivered Him up for us all, how shall He not with Him also freely give us all things? Who shall bring a charge against God's elect? It is God who justifies. Who is he who condemns? It is Christ who died, and furthermore is also risen, who is even at the right hand of God, who also makes intercession for us. Who shall separate us from the love of Christ? Shall tribulation, or distress, or persecution, or famine, or nakedness, or peril, or sword? As it is written: "For Your sake we are killed all day long; we are accounted as sheep for the slaughter." Yet in all these things we are more than conquerors through Him who loved us (Romans 8:31-37).

It is no wonder that just a little later in this epistle Paul explodes into praise, adoration, and exaltation of the Lord. It is almost as if he is grasping for words to fully express his wonder toward God.

Oh, the depth of the riches both of the wisdom and knowledge of God! How unsearchable are His judgments and His ways past finding out! For who has known the mind of the Lord? Or who has become His counselor? Or who has first given to Him and it shall be repaid to him? For of Him and through Him and to Him are all things, to whom be glory forever. Amen (Romans 11:33-36).

Seeing Jesus—The Image of the Invisible God

The apostle Paul records a prayer he gave for the Colossian Christians in which he prayed that they would "be filled with the knowledge of His will...walk worthy of the Lord...and increasing in the knowledge of God" (Col. 1:9-10). His desire was that the Colossians would have insight into the mystery of the unsearchable riches of Christ. He wanted them to increase in the knowledge of God. He then unfolds these astonishing statements about Jesus:

He is the image of the invisible God, the firstborn over all creation.
For by Him all things were created that are in heaven and that are
on earth, visible and invisible, whether thrones or dominions or prin-
cipalities or powers. All things were created through Him and for
Him. And He is before all things, and in Him all things consist. And
He is the head of the body, the church, who is the beginning, the first-
born from the dead, that in all things He may have the preeminence.
For it pleased the Father that in Him all the fullness should dwell,
and by Him to reconcile all things to Himself, by Him, whether things
on earth or things in heaven, having made peace through the blood
of His cross (Colossians 1:15-20).

Jesus is the image of the invisible God. The first three verses of
Hebrews tells us it is the Son "through whom also [God] made the
worlds" and that He is "the brightness of His glory and the express
image of His person." That is, Jesus is the exact representation of His
nature. In fact, Jesus Himself said, "If you had known Me, you would
have known My Father also..." and "...He who has seen Me has seen the
Father..." (John 14:7,9).

This word *image* in Colossians 1:15 comes from the Greek word
eikon (i-kone'), which is where we get today's term *icon*. It means a like-
ness, a profile, or a representation of something. It is the word that is
used in what is called "representative art." This is art in which a figure
or design in painting or sculpture is meant to represent something that
is real in the physical realm. This "image" represents to the viewer what
is actually and readily existent in another realm. In other words, Jesus
came to give us a physical, actual, and literal image of who God is.

The words *express image*, as used in the Hebrews reference, refer to
the Greek word *charakter* (khar-ak-tare'), which is an engraver's term
meaning a figure stamped with an image—an exact copy or representation. Thus, the Hebrews reference means that Jesus is the exact stamp of
the reality of God, the Father, and the perfect essence of who the Father
literally is.

If you want to know about God, you need look no further than
Jesus; He is the express image of His person, the exact representation of
His nature. He is the fullness of God in bodily form. The fullness of what
God is really like is revealed through Jesus. Some have naively assumed
that Jesus is only the New Testament representation of God. Actually,
He is all that He is all the time. He always has been and always will be.
In the Book of Revelation, He is described to the apostle John as "the
Alpha and the Omega, the Beginning and the End" (Rev. 1:8). Jesus today

is the same Jesus who was and is to come. He "is the same yesterday, today, and forever" (Heb. 13:8).

John begins his Gospel from a different vantage point than the others. He begins his account, not from the historic point of Jesus' entry into the human race, but rather all the way back into eternity past, and there we still find Jesus. He says:

> *In the beginning was the Word, and the Word was with God, and the Word was God. He was in the beginning with God. All things were made through Him, and without Him nothing was made that was made. ... And the Word became flesh and dwelt among us, and we beheld His glory, the glory as of the only begotten of the Father, full of grace and truth* (John 1:1-3,14).

We see that Jesus was preexistent with the Father and, in fact, was the Creator of all things. The Colossians' passage goes on further to say: "For by Him all things were created that are in heaven and that are on earth, visible and invisible, whether thrones or dominions or principalities or powers. All things were created through Him and for Him" (Col. 1:16). Not only did He create all things that exist, but they were created *for* Him.

"So why belabor the point?" you might ask. To know the real Jesus is absolutely critical to our lives and eternal destiny. To place our confidence in some false representation of Jesus will only grant our adversary, the devil, opportunity to deceive and destroy us. We must realize that there certainly are some false representations of Jesus in our culture today. Jesus Himself warned that in the last days false christs and false prophets would arise. It is our job to reveal the true Jesus that those who hear might believe in Him.

While working in a private counseling clinic a number of years ago, a dear elderly lady came to me presenting a certain ailment that the doctors concluded had no physiological cause, yet the woman had continuous pain in her head. Through interviewing the woman over a period of weeks, I compiled her history of involvement in various doctrines and groups. It began to be evident to me she had no solid understanding of the real Jesus, for she had spent time in Mormonism, then in certain Pentecostal denominations. She had gone from group to group, yet she sincerely wanted to be a Christian. She also told of a series of "spiritual" experiences she had encountered through her life. As was my custom in my counseling practice, I led her in a prayer at the conclusion of our sessions, and several times when I did so, she began to shake in a peculiar way when I called upon the name of the Lord Jesus.

About the third time this occurred, I began to perceive this was not a "Holy Spirit" type of spiritual experience. I know you may be thinking that some of us are just slow, but, you guessed it, I was watching a counterfeit spiritual experience. Oh, what need we have in this day of resurging spiritual phenomena for accurate discernment! In this case, when I specifically called out and exposed a spirit of "false spiritual experience," she began to shake violently. When I named "false Jesus," the dear lady began to growl and hiss at me. *Ha! a live one!* I thought to myself. Well, the dear lady was delivered from this insidious deceiver and was at the same time instantly delivered from her physical ailment. Glory to Jesus who is God the Son, the express image of the heavenly Father. It is essential we know the one true God! What need there is for a revelation of the truth about who Jesus is!

Chapter 2

Fixing Our Eyes on Jesus– The Savior of Man

We saw in the last chapter that Jesus is the express image of the Father and God's gracious gift to man. Scriptures are full of deeper glimpses into who He is and what He has done. For example, we read in the Book of Hebrews:

Therefore, since we have so great a cloud of witnesses surrounding us, let us also lay aside every encumbrance, and the sin which so easily entangles us, and let us run with endurance the race that is set before us, fixing our eyes on Jesus, the author and perfecter of faith, who for the joy set before Him endured the cross, despising the shame, and has sat down at the right hand of the throne of God (Hebrews 12:1-2 NAS).

Jesus as the Author and Finisher of Our Faith

Hebrews tells us that Jesus Himself is the author of our faith and the finisher of our faith. What does this mean? The word *author* means "commencement, beginning, the originator, the beginning point, the provocation of." As author, Jesus is the commencement, the beginning, the originator, the beginning point, and the provocation of our faith. As finisher, He is the completer, the consummator, the One who brings to completion, to maturity, to perfection. Jesus is the focus of our faith, the originator of our faith, the object of our faith, and the reason our faith is in existence.

Of course, faith is only as valuable as the object of our faith. I was once in an Alcoholics Anonymous meeting where a cynical addict was saying his "higher power" was a doorknob. He was looking for something outside of himself to deliver him from his addiction. Of course, faith itself didn't work in his case. Although faith is certainly a strong motivation and can move us toward confident action, misplaced faith can be disastrous. As believers, our faith is placed in Jesus, and the strength of our faith is tied up in our perception of Jesus. We need to fix our eyes, gaze intently, and see in a much greater way He who is the originator and perfecter of our faith.

The more that we know of Him, His exceedingly great power, His love that surpasses knowledge, and His kind intentions toward us, the more our faith will grow. Our faith is limited by the smallness of our perception of Him! That is why Paul the apostle's prayer for the Ephesian church was:

> *That Christ may dwell in your hearts through faith; that you, being rooted and grounded in love, may be able to comprehend with all the saints what is the width and length and depth and height—to know the love of Christ which passes knowledge; that you may be filled with all the fullness of God. Now to Him who is able to do exceedingly abundantly above all that we ask or think, according to the power that works in us, to Him be glory in the church by Christ Jesus to all generations, forever and ever. Amen* (Ephesians 3:17-21).

Our knowledge of His power and His greatness gives us confidence in His ability to do what we ask. We can come to know that He can do it for He is omnipotent. But the next question is, is He willing? It is in knowing His love and His kind intentions toward us that we grow in faith and confidence in His willingness to meet us at our point of need and show Himself strong on our behalf. Therefore, He has also revealed Himself to us as our loving Shepherd.

Seeing Jesus as the Shepherd of Our Soul

King David, a shepherd himself, wrote by divine inspiration that the Lord was his Shepherd. The nature of a shepherd is revealed in his great twenty-third psalm:

> *The Lord is my shepherd; I shall not want. He makes me to lie down in green pastures; He leads me beside the still waters. He restores my soul; He leads me in the paths of righteousness for His name's sake. Yea, though I walk through the valley of the shadow of death, I will fear no evil; for You are with me; Your rod and Your staff, they comfort me. You prepare a table before me in the presence of my enemies;*

You anoint my head with oil; my cup runs over. Surely goodness and mercy shall follow me all the days of my life; and I will dwell in the house of the Lord forever.

The Lord is a caring Shepherd to us. Jesus affirmed that in His teaching in the Gospel of John. He stated: "I am the good shepherd. The good shepherd gives His life for the sheep" (Jn. 10:11) and "I am the good shepherd; and I know My sheep, and am known by My own" (Jn. 10:14).

We see from these Scriptures the intention of the Lord to meet our needs. David said that because he had the Lord as his Shepherd, he had no want. He was led into places of peace and provision. The good Shepherd brought him to green pastures and still waters. He was his protection and comfort from the threat of evil.

A shepherd is one who protects, corrects, guides, and provides. The description of the job of the shepherd can be extracted from the words of the prophet in Ezekiel chapter 34. This passage tells us that the shepherd will feed the flock, strengthen them, gather them, heal them, bind up the broken, and protect them from harm. The Scripture goes on to say that where the shepherds of Israel failed to do these things, the Lord Himself would come and be our Shepherd.

For thus says the Lord God: "Indeed I Myself will search for My sheep and seek them out. As a shepherd seeks out his flock on the day he is among his scattered sheep, so will I seek out My sheep and deliver them from all the places where they were scattered on a cloudy and dark day. ... I will feed My flock, and I will make them lie down," says the Lord God. "I will seek what was lost and bring back what was driven away, bind up the broken and strengthen what was sick; but I will destroy the fat and the strong, and feed them in judgment." (Ezekiel 34:11-12,15-16).

Part of the Lord's shepherding care is that He will give us pastors who will carry His heart for His flock. We see the promise of a shepherd in Jeremiah 3:14-15:

"Return, O backsliding children," says the Lord; "for I am married to you. I will take you, one from a city and two from a family, and I will bring you to Zion. And I will give you shepherds according to My heart, who will feed you with knowledge and understanding."

A pastor is the expression of the individual care that Jesus has for His flock. More will be said about this in Section II of this book. But the primary point here is that Jesus Himself is the Chief Shepherd and truly cares for our soul.

Second, we each have Him as our personal Shepherd. Certainly Scripture teaches a concept that He has given pastors, or "under shepherds," to lead and guide the flock, but He remains the Chief Shepherd. Leaders who have the responsibility to lead and guide must always understand the built-in limitation that this implies. The under shepherd, or anyone else who speaks as an oracle from God, must never usurp the position the Chief Shepherd has in a believer's life. In fact, it is the under shepherd's job to lead believers to Jesus and to encourage each sheep to hear from God directly.

Keys to Hearing the Shepherd's Voice

Hearing God's "voice" is an important part of every believer's experience. Scripture teaches that every believer should be able to "hear" His voice. I believe this means that every believer should be able to receive communication from God in such a way that the individual will know that the message is from Him. In John 10, Jesus described the kind of relationship we should have with Him. "I am the good shepherd; the good shepherd lays down His life for the sheep. ... I am the good shepherd; and I know My own, and My own know Me. ... My sheep hear My voice, and I know them, and they follow Me" (John 10:11,14,27 NAS).

Hearing God's voice should be the normal experience for a follower of Jesus. In chapter 15 of the Gospel of John, Jesus also says, "No longer do I call you servants, for a servant does not know what his master is doing; but I have called you friends, for all things that I heard from My Father I have made known to you" (Jn. 15:15). He wants to reveal to us information from the Father. Later, He states, "...Everyone who is of the truth hears My voice" (Jn. 18:37). In fact, it is by hearing God's voice, His *rhema* word, that we are nourished and fed: "It is written, 'Man shall not live by bread alone, but by every word that proceeds from the mouth of God' " (Mt. 4:4). The ability to hear God's voice is critical to successful living as a Christian.

I believe leaders can and should train every believer to receive guidance from the Lord. But our ability to hear can be sharpened or dulled by one critical factor that has to do with our attitude of heart, and that is a willingness to obey what we hear. To listen with a heart to obey is critical to hearing properly. To listen and then to do what He tells you is key to a continuous flow of communication. When we hear a directive from God, we have, at that time, an option; we can respond to the light He has given us and He will give us more light, or we can hesitate, and the light will fade.

This principle is shown in Jesus' words in John 12:35: "...Walk while you have the light, lest darkness overtake you; he who walks in darkness does not know where he is going." The process goes like this: First, we hear from God. Second, we obey what light He has given. Third, we are given more. The sad truth is that the other trend goes as follows: First, we hear from God. Second, after we have heard from God, we either ignore or outright disobey His directive. Third, we will lose the light that we had opportunity to walk in. Finally, we then begin to lose the things that we had already attained to.

The spiritual principle at work is stated more clearly in Mark 4:23-25 (KJV): "If any man have ears to hear, let him hear. And He said unto them, Take heed what ye hear: with what measure ye mete, it shall be measured to you: and unto you that hear shall more be given. For he that hath, to him shall be given: and he that hath not, from him shall be taken even that which he hath."

So to hear with a heart to obey is the key to hearing more, and if we disobey, Scripture tells us that even what we already have will be taken away. Oh, how important it is then to hear and obey. In fact, it is at this point that something the Scriptures call a "spirit of slumber" begins to set in. This is described in Romans 10 and 11 as something that happened to the children of Israel when they continued to be disobedient to God's Word. "But to Israel He saith, All day long I have stretched forth My hands unto a disobedient and gainsaying people. ... (According as it is written, God hath given them the spirit of slumber, eyes that they should not see, and ears that they should not hear)" (Rom. 10:21; 11:8 KJV).

While in the state of spiritual slumber, many Christians continue to go through their religious routines, but after awhile, even spiritual activities begin to seem dull, boring, and even burdensome. Though having ears, they do not hear. They find themselves not receiving the nourishment, strengthening, or encouragement that comes from hearing God's voice. It is at this point that spiritual famine or drought sets in.

When we discover ourselves in that state of spiritual slumber, we are ready for a wake-up call. We are ready to hear His voice once again. It is when we get hungry enough and thirsty enough and we begin to want to hear His voice once again that He will instruct us once again what it is He wants us to do. The great Shepherd of our soul will seek us out and speak once again. At this point, the cycle of opportunity to hear and obey begins again. It is then we need to be as the prophet of old in Isaiah 50:4-5 (NIV):

The Sovereign Lord has given me an instructed tongue, to know the word that sustains the weary. He wakens me morning by morning, wakens my ear to listen like one being taught. The Sovereign Lord has opened my ears, and I have not been rebellious; I have not drawn back.

Seeing Jesus as Prince of Peace

Isaiah the prophet spoke of Jesus in this manner:

For unto us a Child is born, unto us a Son is given; and the govern-ment will be upon His shoulder. And His name will be called Won-derful, Counselor, Mighty God, Everlasting Father, Prince of Peace. Of the increase of His government and peace there will be no end, upon the throne of David and over His kingdom, to order it and establish it with judgment and justice from that time forward, even forever. The zeal of the Lord of hosts will perform this (Isaiah 9:6-7).

Peace is in contrast to war. There is actually a violent war going on around us and against us. Jesus did not promise us exemption from the fight. The enemy of our soul has come to do us harm. He wants to steal, kill, and destroy (see Jn. 10:10). But Jesus came to bring peace to all who place their trust in Him. Jesus told us: "Peace I leave with you, My peace I give to you; not as the world gives do I give to you. Let not your heart be troubled, neither let it be afraid" (Jn. 14:27). Jesus did promise us He would be our Mighty Warrior and Prince of Peace. Wherever He rules, there is peace. His government brings peace. In fact, the Kingdom of God is described in Romans 14:17 as righteousness, peace, and joy in the Holy Spirit. The fact that Jesus promised us peace, however, is the very indicator that there is turmoil without Him. This is His promise:

These things I have spoken to you, that in Me you may have peace. In the world you will have tribulation; but be of good cheer, I have overcome the world (John 16:33).

In one incident, we saw Jesus assert His peace over the adversary as well as over the very forces of nature when He rescued His disciples from a violent storm. The prince of the power of the air had stirred up a mighty wind. Without Jesus, the disciples would have perished.

Then He arose and rebuked the wind, and said to the sea, "Peace, be still!" And the wind ceased and there was a great calm (Mark 4:39).

We have an adversary who will attempt to bring us torment and tribulation. But we often blame our troubles and turmoil in life on God when we should be placing blame on the one to whom blame is due. We must understand the nature of this battle. The Lord is our peace because

He is at war with our adversary. Romans 16:20 shows this contrast very clearly: "And the God of peace will crush satan under your feet shortly. The grace of our Lord Jesus Christ be with you." That is why we need to understand that our Lord is also a consuming fire.

Seeing Jesus as a Refiner's Fire

We have a Savior who is also a consuming fire. It was said of Him in Malachi 3:1-3:

> *"Behold, I send My messenger, and he will prepare the way before Me. And the Lord, whom you seek, will suddenly come to His temple, Even the Messenger of the covenant, in whom you delight. Behold, He is coming," says the Lord of hosts. "But who can endure the day of His coming? And who can stand when He appears? For He is like a refiner's fire and like launderer's soap. He will sit as a refiner and a purifier of silver; He will purify the sons of Levi, and purge them as gold and silver, that they may offer to the Lord an offering in righteousness."*

I will have to admit that I am, like most, guilty at times of selective hearing. That is, I have certain Scriptures I like and others that I "conveniently" overlook. But the Scriptures are as a sharp two-edged sword, cutting in two directions at once (see Heb. 4:12). Most truth in Scripture can be found to have a counterbalancing truth somewhere else in Scripture, designed by God to keep us honest. So is the case with our examination of Jesus.

A prolonged examination of Jesus, such as we are doing, must reveal Him to be both grand and dreadful. He is grand to those who love and put their trust in Him, but at the same time, He is dreadful to His adversaries. He is a loving God and a gracious Savior, but He is also a consuming fire as is plainly spoken in Hebrews 12:28-29:

> *Therefore, since we are receiving a kingdom which cannot be shaken, let us have grace, by which we may serve God acceptably with reverence and godly fear. For our God is a consuming fire.*

The fact that our Lord is a dreaded warrior is great when we consider His vengeance against our adversaries. But one of the Scriptures that should strike fear into our heart is the section of Hebrews 10 where we see a warning for those who despise the Lord's gift of grace:

> *Therefore, brethren, having boldness to enter the Holiest by the blood of Jesus, by a new and living way which He consecrated for us, through the veil, that is, His flesh, and having a High Priest over the house of God, let us draw near with a true heart in full assurance of*

faith, having our hearts sprinkled from an evil conscience and our bodies washed with pure water. Let us hold fast the confession of our hope without wavering, for He who promised is faithful. And let us consider one another in order to stir up love and good works, not forsaking the assembling of ourselves together, as is the manner of some, but exhorting one another, and so much the more as you see the Day approaching. For if we sin willfully after we have received the knowledge of the truth, there no longer remains a sacrifice for sins, but a certain fearful expectation of judgment, and fiery indignation which will devour the adversaries. Anyone who has rejected Moses' law dies without mercy on the testimony of two or three witnesses. Of how much worse punishment, do you suppose, will he be thought worthy who has trampled the Son of God underfoot, counted the blood of the covenant by which he was sanctified a common thing, and insulted the Spirit of grace? For we know Him who said, "Vengeance is Mine, I will repay," says the Lord. And again, "The Lord will judge His people." It is a fearful thing to fall into the hands of the living God (Hebrews 10:19-31).

Chapter 3

Fixing Our Eyes on Jesus— The Lion of the Tribe of Judah

The "Lamb" Is a "Lion"

Then I saw a strong angel proclaiming with a loud voice, "Who is worthy to open the scroll and to loose its seals?" And no one in heaven or on the earth or under the earth was able to open the scroll, or to look at it. So I wept much, because no one was found worthy to open and read the scroll, or to look at it. But one of the elders said to me, "Do not weep. Behold, the Lion of the tribe of Judah, the Root of David, has prevailed to open the scroll and to loose its seven seals." And I looked, and behold, in the midst of the throne and of the four living creatures, and in the midst of the elders, stood a Lamb as though it had been slain, having seven horns and seven eyes, which are the seven Spirits of God sent out into all the earth (Revelation 5:2-6).

In Revelation chapter 5 we see Jesus described as the Lion from the Tribe of Judah. In this prophetic book, He is a Lion who appears to John as a Lamb who was slain. He is actually one and the same. I believe there is coming an increase of insight into this aspect of the nature of our Lord Jesus who is the Lamb of God and yet a Lion from Judah's tribe. *Judah* means praise. We know King David of the tribe of Judah, the forerunner of Jesus our King, as the worshiping warrior. We have known Jesus as the Lamb of God, our Savior, but soon we will see Him manifested as a Lion, a ferocious Warrior and the King and Judge of all the earth. This Lamb who was slain is being called a Lion in this passage from Revelation, and He is the only One worthy to open the seven seals of judgment. He is about to be revealed as Ruler and Judge. With that revelation will also come the realization that the last-days church is being called with Him and through Him into that same role of ruler and judge as described in these next verses from chapter 5:

> *And they sang a new song, saying: "You are worthy to take the scroll, and to open its seals; for You were slain, and have redeemed us to God by Your blood out of every tribe and tongue and people and nation, and have made us kings and priests to our God; and we shall reign on the earth"* (Revelation 5:9-10).

In Chapter 6 we see Him as the One who will execute judgment. The following excerpts show Him as such. Chapters 6 through 8 go on to tell of the unfolding of these seals of judgment.

> *When He opened the fifth seal, I saw under the altar the souls of those who had been slain for the word of God and for the testimony which they held. And they cried with a loud voice, saying, "How long, O Lord, holy and true, until You judge and avenge our blood on those who dwell on the earth?" ... And the kings of the earth, the great men, the rich men, the commanders, the mighty men, every slave and every free man, hid themselves in the caves and in the rocks of the mountains, and said to the mountains and rocks, "Fall on us and hide us from the face of Him who sits on the throne and from the wrath of the Lamb! For the great day of His wrath has come, and who is able to stand?"* (Revelation 6:9-10,15-17)

The Lord is about to show Himself as a man of war.

> *Now I saw heaven opened, and behold, a white horse. And He who sat on him was called Faithful and True, and in righteousness He judges and makes war* (Revelation 19:11).

> *The Lord will go forth like a warrior, He will arouse His zeal like a man of war. He will utter a shout, yes, He will raise a war cry* [KJV— roar]. *He will prevail against His enemies* (Isaiah 42:13 NAS).

The prophet Joel, whose prophetic words apply directly to the end times, show a "last-days" Jesus roaring as a Lion who calls His saints to war as well.

The Lord also will roar from Zion, and utter His voice from Jerusalem; the heavens and earth will shake; but the Lord will be a shelter for His people, and the strength of the children of Israel. "So you shall know that I am the Lord your God, dwelling in Zion My holy mountain. Then Jerusalem shall be holy, and no aliens shall ever pass through her again" (Joel 3:16-17).

Joel 2:28-29 describes the days we are currently in: "And it shall come to pass afterward that I will pour out My Spirit on all flesh; your sons and your daughters shall prophesy, your old men shall dream dreams, your young men shall see visions. And also on My menservants and on My maidservants I will pour out My Spirit in those days."

It is in this context that we begin Joel chapter 3, and so we need to see Joel 3 as a very significant Scripture for us as we come to the end of the age. This chapter describes the happenings that will be going on "in those days and at that time" (Joel 3:1). We see that this will be a significant time of battle, as the Lord comes forth as our Lion, our Mighty Warrior. Here we see Him calling us to the battle as well.

Proclaim this among the nations: "Prepare for war! Wake up the mighty men, let all the men of war draw near, let them come up. Beat your plowshares into swords and your pruning hooks into spears; let the weak say, 'I am strong.' " Assemble and come, all you nations, and gather together all around. Cause Your mighty ones to go down there, O Lord. "Let the nations be wakened, and come up to the Valley of Jehoshaphat; for there I will sit to judge all the surrounding nations. Put in the sickle, for the harvest is ripe. Come, go down; for the winepress is full, the vats overflow—for their wickedness is great" (Joel 3:9-13).

The valley of Jehoshaphat is the valley of judgment. It is also significant because it is where the enemy of Israel was defeated through praises to God (see 2 Chron. 20). Praise is a weapon of war because praise arouses the Lord to a place of zeal. Praise releases judgment against our enemies. It is as we praise Him that He becomes full of zeal for His house. The Lord's triumphal entry to Jerusalem, as the crowd praised Him, saying, "Hosanna to the Son of David! 'Blessed is He who comes in the name of the Lord!' Hosanna in the highest!" awakened in Him a readiness to judge and cleanse His temple (see Mt. 21:7-16).

Psalm 149 also connects the function of praise with the function of warfare and tells us this is the responsibility of all His saints.

Let the high praises of God be in their mouth, and a two-edged sword in their hand, to execute vengeance on the nations, and punishments on the peoples; to bind their kings with chains, and their nobles with fetters of iron; to execute on them the written judgment–this honor have all His saints. Praise the Lord! (Psalm 149:6-9)

When we lift up Jesus, we participate in the battle through our praise of the Lord. When He is lifted up, our enemies flee. He has called us to battle, but our battle is not against flesh and blood (see Eph. 6:12). Our weapons are not natural, but they are powerful through God to the pulling down of spiritual strongholds (see 2 Cor. 10:3-4). Praises to Jesus are a weapon of war. When we give Him the praise He is worthy of, He goes to war on our behalf. When we acknowledge Him as our Mighty Warrior, He will fight for us. He is the Lord, mighty in battle (see Ps. 24:8).

The Lord and His Kingdom

...until the appearing of our Lord Jesus Christ, which He will bring about at the proper time–He who is the blessed and only Sovereign, the King of kings and Lord of lords; who alone possesses immortality and dwells in unapproachable light; whom no man has seen or can see. To Him be honor and eternal dominion! Amen (1 Timothy 6:14-16 NAS).

Then Jesus went about all the cities and villages, teaching in their synagogues, preaching the gospel of the kingdom, and healing every sickness and every disease among the people (Matthew 9:35).

Then He called His twelve disciples together and gave them power and authority over all demons, and to cure diseases. He sent them to preach the kingdom of God and to heal the sick (Luke 9:1-2).

The message that Jesus preached was the gospel of the Kingdom of God. A simple definition of a *kingdom* is "a domain where a king rules." The term *Kingdom of God* implies a King, and Jesus is that King. Not only did Jesus preach the Kingdom of God, but His disciples were instructed to preach the Kingdom. In fact, Jesus connected the accomplishment of the church's mission to the full declaration of the gospel of the Kingdom to all the nations as a witness before the end would come (see Mt. 24:14). More about the nature, power, and authority of this Kingdom is addressed later, but the purpose of this chapter is to focus on the King of the Kingdom. Simply put, wherever Jesus has rule, there the Kingdom has come.

David caught a glimpse of this King and wrote of Him in Psalm 2.

Why do the nations rage, and the people plot a vain thing? The kings of the earth set themselves, and the rulers take counsel together, against the Lord and against His Anointed, saying ... "Yet I have set My King on My holy hill of Zion. I will declare the decree: The Lord has said to Me, 'You are My Son, today I have begotten You. Ask of Me, and I will give You the nations for Your inheritance, and the ends of the earth for Your possession.' " ... Now therefore, be wise, O kings; be instructed, you judges of the earth. Serve the Lord with fear, and rejoice with trembling. Kiss the Son, lest He be angry, and you perish in the way, when His wrath is kindled but a little. Blessed are all those who put their trust in Him (Psalm 2:1-2,6-8,10-12).

Daniel saw Him in a night vision.

I was watching in the night visions, and behold, One like the Son of Man, coming with the clouds of heaven! He came to the Ancient of Days, and they brought Him near before Him. Then to Him was given dominion and glory and a kingdom, that all peoples, nations, and languages should serve Him. His dominion is an everlasting dominion, which shall not pass away, and His kingdom the one which shall not be destroyed (Daniel 7:13-14).

At His ascension Jesus said, "All authority in heaven and on earth has been given to Me" (Mt. 28:18 NIV). The implications of that are staggering. His supreme rule extends over all. He rules over space. He rules over time and eternity. He rules over nature. And although there are pockets of rebellion currently remaining in the hearts of men, His rule shall eventually and inevitably extend to every individual, for Scripture states in Philippians 2:10-11 (TLB) that "at the name of Jesus every knee shall bow...and that every tongue shall confess that Jesus Christ is Lord, to the glory of God the Father." Romans 10:9 states, "...if you confess with your mouth the Lord Jesus and believe in your heart that God has raised Him from the dead, you will be saved." The acknowledgment of Jesus as Lord is directly connected to His saving grace, but I am convinced many people don't fully understand the significance of the statement that Jesus is Lord.

The Lordship of Jesus Christ is apparently one of the most neglected and least understood aspects of Jesus. As incredible as that statement sounds, the lack of understanding of His Lordship is clearly evident in the lives of many who claim to be Christians, as evidenced by the general lack of response to it in the lives of those who claim Him as their Savior.

For example, in the religious "Bible belt" region of the country in which I live, polls state that a phenomenal 83 percent of the population believe in a literal physical return of Jesus to the earth. Yet the most casual observer can easily conclude there is a vast difference between a owledge about Jesus and a faith in Him that produces changed lives.

At the same time, Scripture points to the fact that a belief about Jesus as Savior is not the same as a surrender to Jesus as Lord. In fact, one very grave problem within western Christianity has become an "easy believism" that is void of repentance and Lordship. It is "faith" without repentance, "salvation" without sanctification, "mental assent" without life-changing surrender. He is not a Savior whom we have the option of establishing as Lord of our lives; rather, as we acknowledge Him as Lord, He will save us.

In our zeal to be theologically "proper" regarding the grand theme of grace, modern Christianity has often been guilty of presenting a "gospel" of faith without Lordship, a cheap "grace" that's not really grace but *licentiousness* (which means absence of restraint, indecency, wantonness—note Jude 1:4: "For certain persons have crept in unnoticed, those who were long beforehand marked out for this condemnation, ungodly persons who turn the grace of our God into licentiousness and deny our only Master and Lord, Jesus Christ" [NAS]).

This "grace" is justification of sin without repentance on the part of the sinner. It is the preaching of forgiveness without requiring repentance. It is church membership without church discipline, communion without confession, faith without action. It is desiring to have Jesus as Savior but not as Lord, wanting Him to save us but not to rule over our lives. Costly grace recognizes the call to discipleship that Jesus expects in light of our redemption.

Christ gave all for us and expects nothing less in return. Our relationship with Him is the "treasure in a field" for which a man sells all he has to purchase. It is the costly pearl a man gives all to acquire. It is the call of Jesus for which a disciple leaves his nets, forsakes all, and follows. Such a gospel demands total surrender. It says, "If you receive Me as Lord, I will save you." It is costly because it costs us our life, but it is redemption because in exchange we gain that which is true life, that which is eternal.

Part of the problem is the lack of understanding of exactly what it means to acknowledge Jesus as Lord. In the Old Testament, the term *Lord* referred to a word from the root word meaning, "to rule, sovereign, controller, master, owner." Throughout the Old Testament, there is the clear declaration that there is only one Lord and God. He is the Lord of Heaven. He is the Lord who ruled over the flood. He rules sovereignly as King over all His creation, including the expanse of the galaxies; the entire realm of the heavenly hosts; the domain of fallen angels whose fate is already sealed; the domain of the earth, encompassing the ecosystems of the earth; plants and animals. But we also discover that God as Lord and Sovereign has two aspects: First, He is Lord over all creation and universe. This, however, did not include the domain of the heart of man. That domain was betrayed to the enemy through the fall of man. We were enslaved to sin; we could not choose.

Although He rules sovereignly over all His creation, this one domain had, for a time, eluded His Lordship, but only by sovereign permission. That domain was the heart and volition of man; it was the "world system" that was created by man that man had, in turn, betrayed to the evil one.

Then came Jesus! We find Jesus introduced as Lord and referred to as Lord close to 3,000 times in the New Testament. Jesus demonstrated His Lordship—His rulership over creation—by turning water to wine, through multiplying bread and fish, even through displaying His authority over the elements. He commanded the wind and waves. He exerted authority over demons and the domain of darkness and over sickness and disease.

He was the Lord God, who now had interposed His presence into the human condition in the form of Jesus, the Son of God. The Scripture indicates that Jesus came to intervene, and through His coming, He bought back that one last, lost domain, thus being established as Lord of all, once and for all.

This final dimension of His Lordship is clearly stated in Acts and Philippians:

> *Therefore let all the house of Israel know assuredly that God has made this Jesus, whom you crucified, both Lord and Christ* (Act 2:36).

> *Have this attitude in yourselves which was also in Christ Jesus, who, although He existed in the form of God, did not regard equality with God a thing to be grasped, but emptied Himself, taking the form of a bond-servant, and being made in the likeness of men. And being found in appearance as a man, He humbled Himself by becoming obedient to the point of death, even death on a cross. Therefore also God highly exalted Him, and bestowed on Him the name which is above every name, that at the name of Jesus EVERY KNEE SHOULD BOW, of those who are in heaven, and on earth, and under the earth, and that every tongue should confess that Jesus Christ is Lord, to the glory of God the Father* (Philippians 2:5-11 NAS).

This final establishment of Jesus as Lord by the Father—even over the hearts of every man—gives the conclusion of the matter. He is Lord of all. We are all destined to acknowledge it by the confession of our tongue and the bending of our knee. Acknowledging Him as Lord implies putting faith in His saving power, while giving Him right to rule over our lives. It is a gospel that includes repentance *and* faith. The fact is that everyone *will* acknowledge Him as Lord. Every individual may do so willingly now, for which there is great benefit, or under duress at the final judgment, in which case there will be great remorse. Nevertheless, He is Lord!

This King Is Also a Priest

It is important to add that the rule of King Jesus is a rule of love. The greatest news for us in light of His Lordship is that this King is also a merciful priest.

Hebrews 4:14-16 states:

Seeing then that we have a great High Priest who has passed through the heavens, Jesus the Son of God, let us hold fast our confession. For we do not have a High Priest who cannot sympathize with our weaknesses, but was in all points tempted as we are, yet without sin. Let us therefore come boldly to the throne of grace, that we may obtain mercy and find grace to help in time of need.

Hebrews 10:19-23 goes on to say:

Therefore, brethren, having boldness to enter the Holiest by the blood of Jesus, by a new and living way which He consecrated for us, through the veil, that is, His flesh, and having a High Priest over the house of God, let us draw near with a true heart in full assurance of faith, having our hearts sprinkled from an evil conscience and our bodies washed with pure water. Let us hold fast the confession of our hope without wavering, for He who promised is faithful.

Oh, how wonderful is our kind, compassionate King Jesus! He is a dreaded Judge to those who rebel, but how excellent is His benevolent rule over us who believe. Words are often insufficient to fully describe this glorious God of ours. The following attempt to describe our King was adapted from a sermon given a number of years ago by S.M. Lockridge.

"The Bible says Jesus is the King of Kings and the Lord of Lords.

"He's a seven way King. He's the King of the Jews, He's the King of Israel, The King of Righteousness. He's the King of the Ages. He's the King of Heaven. He's the King of Glory, the King of kings and Lord of lords.

"David says the heavens declare the glory of God and the firmament showeth His handiwork. This King is an inexorable king. No means of measure can define His limitless love. No barrier can hinder Him from pouring out His blessings. He's enduringly strong. He's entirely sincere. He's eternally steadfast. He's immortally graceful. He's imperially powerful. He's impartially merciful.

"He's the greatest phenomenon that has ever crossed the horizon of this world. He's God's Son. He's a sinner's Savior. He's the centerpiece of civilization. He's unique. He's unparalleled. He's unprecedented. He's supreme. He's pre-eminent. He's the loftiest idea in literature. He's the highest personality in philosophy. He's the fundamental doctrine of true theology. He's the cardinal necessity of spiritual religion. He's the miracle of the age. He's the superlative of everything good that you choose to call Him. Well, He's the only one able to supply all of our needs simultaneously.

"He supplies strength for the weak. He is available for the tempted and tried. He sympathizes and He saves. He strengthens and He sustains. He guards and He guides. He heals the sick. He cleanses the lepers. He forgives sinners. He discharges debtors. He delivers the captives. He defends the feeble. He blesses the young. He serves the unfortunate. He regards the aged. He rewards the diligent, and He beautifies the meek.

"This King is the key to knowledge. He's the well spring of wisdom. He's the doorway of deliverance. He is the pathway to peace. He's the roadway of righteousness. He is the highway of holiness. He's the gateway of glory. He's the Master of the mighty. He's the captain of the conquerors. He's the head of the heroes. He's the leader of the legislators. He's the overseer of the overcomers. He's the Governor of governors. He's the Prince of princes. He's the King of kings, and He's the Lord of lords.

"Well. That's my King Jesus. My King, His office is manifold. His promise is sure. His life is matchless. His goodness is limitless. His mercy is everlasting. His love never changes. His word is enough. His grace is sufficient. His reign is righteous. His yoke is easy and His burden is light.

"Well, I wish I could describe Him to you. He's indescribable. He's indescribable, yeah. He's incomprehensible. He's invincible. He's irresistible. I'm trying to tell you, the heavens of heavens cannot contain Him, let alone a man explain Him. You can't get Him out of your mind. You can't get Him off of your hands. Well, You can't outlive Him, and you can't live without Him.

"Well, Pharisees couldn't stand Him, but they also found out, they couldn't stop Him. Pilate couldn't fault Him. The witnesses couldn't get their testimonies to agree. Herod couldn't kill Him. Death couldn't handle Him, and the grave couldn't hold Him. That's my King. Yes! He always has been, and He always will be. I'm telling you, He had no predecessor, and He'll have no successor. There was nobody before Him, and there'll be nobody after Him. You can't impeach Him, and He's not going to resign. That's Jesus! That's our King! To Him belongs the Kingdom and the Power and the Glory, forever and ever and ever and ever! Amen! and Amen! and Amen!!"[1]

---

1. Transcribed from the sermon tape, "Jesus Is a Seven-Way King," and used by permission of Institute in Basic Life Principles, Box One, Oak Brook, IL, 60522. Punctuation is author's own.

Section II

The Structure Defined

...and upon this rock I will build My church; and the gates of hell shall not prevail against it (Matthew 16:18 KJV).

Having been built on the foundation of the apostles and prophets, Jesus Christ Himself being the chief corner stone (Ephesians 2:20).

Chapter 4

What Is "the Church" (And What Isn't)?

The church is in major transition. Most people know that the church, as it has been, is neither satisfactory to God nor adequate to the task before us in these closing days of this present dispensation. Meanwhile, today's world population presents the possibility for a larger harvest of souls than has even been seen in the previous 2,000 years combined. Advances in technology, communications, travel, and education are pressing us to radically change our entire approach to spreading the gospel and our approach to the way that we "do church."

At the same time, since so many are becoming discontented with the status quo and recognizing the need to change, we also find ourselves at a place of unique vulnerability to changing things in a wrong direction. In many cases, the traditional church has become dead and lifeless, yet the reaction is often just as disconcerting, as people leave the traditional churches and spin off into maverick expressions of disorganized independence that are hardly useful to the Lord's overall Kingdom purposes.

It is my opinion that both the traditional ecclesiology and some of the consequent reactions that are emerging in many quarters are wrong. I propose that we entertain the possibility that some of what is being called "the church" is, in fact, not the church when held to the plumbline of Scripture. A return to the scriptural blueprint is needed. At this point, it is essential to state that this does not imply a return to a first-century pattern, but rather, it is a call to a fresh examination of the Scripture for that which is universal and timeless and can be pragmatically applied to this present hour. We need a twenty-first century pattern rooted in the universal truths of Scripture concerning the biblical definition of *church*.

So how does the Scripture define this wondrous thing called "the church"? Some would define it as the universal collective membership of all true believers in Jesus. In fact, Jesus implied this when He stated He would build His *church*—singular (see Mt. 16:18). We need to see all true believers as part of God's family. The fact is, however, that Jesus only mentioned the church one other place in the gospels (see Mt. 18:17), and the implication in this case was that it was a definable local group of believers. By His statement, Jesus established a clearly definable ex-communication process for that local body. He then very clearly states a plural version (churches) in His words to John in the Book of Revelation (see Rev. 2–3).

The Epistles, then, develop the theme of the church. There we find either *church* or *churches* mentioned over 100 times. So, though there is one dimension of truth to the universal church concept, there is just as strong an implication that there are also singular local expressions of the church that are independent, stand-alone churches. These are defined in Scripture in terms of geographically configured local churches. (See Acts 9:31: *"Then the churches throughout all Judea..."* and First Corinthians 16:19: *"The churches of Asia greet you...,"* etc.)

Now the question is, "Does every gathering of Christians constitute a church according to God's definition of things?" Some, who have discarded the organized church, claim for themselves the Scripture from Matthew 18:20 stating, "For where two or three are gathered together in My name, I am there in the midst of them." It is important to note, however, that this Scripture was not meant to be a teaching about the nature of the church. In fact, it is specifically placed in the context of instructions about praying.

However, from this has come an entire movement of people supposing that their small home meetings are actually a church. They may be, but then again, they may not be. We must be cautious to not oversimplify something that an examination of Scripture reveals as being a bit more complex. I propose that there are other factors (factors that are quite apart from the numbers) by which we determine if a gathering is, in fact, a church according to the Scripture.

Let's look specifically at some scriptural descriptions of the church. The following are seven analogies commonly portrayed in Scripture that give us insight into the nature of the church: a sheepfold; a family; a vine; a bride; an army; a spiritual building; a body.

The church as a sheepfold, with Jesus as the Door to the sheepfold and the Shepherd of the sheep, is portrayed in passages such as John 10:1-18. This image has a relational focus upon God and the personal nature of our relationship with Him. This analogy speaks to us of belonging and protection. Scripture teaches a very clear membership to the church. You are clearly in or clearly out. To be "in" is a place of protection and safety.

The church as a family, with God as our Father, Jesus our elder brother, and we as brothers and sisters, is also demonstrated in Scripture: "But as many as received Him, to them He gave the right to become children of God" (Jn. 1:12; see also Mt. 6:9; Eph. 2:19; 3:14-15; Heb. 12:5-9, etc.). The relational focus in this analogy is primarily upon God the Father and our relationship with Him, and secondarily, upon our relationship with one another. This speaks to issues of relationship, fatherhood, and discipline.

The church as a vine, with Jesus as the Vine and ourselves as the branches, is shown in John 15:1-17. In this case, the relational focus is toward Jesus and our ongoing relationship with Him. This speaks of fruitfulness through being connected (and staying connected) to Him.

The church as a bride, with Jesus as the Bridegroom, is established in Ephesians 5:22-32 and Revelation 19:7-8. This analogy has a relational focus toward Jesus and our corporate relationship with Him. This speaks of love, affection, devotion, loyalty, and covenant.

The New Testament also portrays the church as an army with God as the Captain of the Hosts (see 2 Tim. 2:3-7; 2 Cor. 10:3-4; Eph. 6:10-18; Lk. 10:18-19; Rev. 12:9-12, etc.). Here the relational focus is upon our adversary. This picture speaks of spiritual objectives, order, rank, and authority.

The first four pictures of the church primarily focus on our relationship with God. The fifth picture, with the church as an army, deals primarily with our relationship to our adversary. The last two primarily focus on our relationships with one another. These remaining two give us insight into how the church ought to be connected to one another. These are the areas I want to unfold a little deeper in the remainder of this chapter.

The church as a spiritual building has Jesus as the Cornerstone. He is the key frame of reference, the plumbline for the construction of the entire building. This picture has a relational focus toward one another and toward the foundation of the building. It speaks to issues of the "connectedness," the structure of the building, and the unique worship experience that is found there.

> *Now, therefore, you are no longer strangers and foreigners, but fellow citizens with the saints and members of the household of God, having been built on the foundation of the apostles and prophets, Jesus Christ Himself being the chief cornerstone, in whom the whole building, being fitted together, grows into a holy temple in the Lord, in whom you also are being built together for a dwelling place of God in the Spirit* (Ephesians 2:19-22).

> *Coming to Him as to a living stone, rejected indeed by men, but chosen by God and precious, you also, as living stones, are being built up a spiritual house, a holy priesthood, to offer up spiritual sacrifices acceptable to God through Jesus Christ. Therefore it is also contained in the Scripture, "Behold, I lay in Zion a chief cornerstone, elect, precious, and he who believes on Him will by no means be put to shame"* (1 Peter 2:4-6).

Being "joined together" and "built together" into a dwelling of God simply means that we are "connected" by relationship with one another. And God insists that we be rightly related to one another. The Scriptures such as First John 2:9-11 imply that if we want to stay in right relationship with God, we must be about the work of maintaining a right relationship with our brothers and sisters in Christ.

This means that the task of building and maintaining right relationships is not an optional sideline, but rather, it is an essential ingredient of our Christian life. In fact, God is so concerned that we be rightly related to one another that He has inextricably connected His dealings with us to our dealings with one another. For instance, if we don't forgive others, He will not forgive us (see Mk. 11:25-26). The entire law and prophets are summarized in Matthew 22:37-40 as our being rightly related to God and to one another.

When we are gathered together in right relationship to one another, there is a setting for worship that is pleasing to the Lord according to First Peter 2:5. When we get the pattern right, there dwells a unique or special manifestation of God's presence (see Ex. 29:43-46).

So, in order for a building to be built, each brick must fit into its proper place and "connect" to the other bricks. The mortar is love and commitment. It also necessitates a proper foundation. Being rightly related speaks as well to the issue of proper structure and government within the church. Being rightly fitted and held together includes understanding how to relate to spiritual authority and how to properly exercise spiritual authority.

Since Scripture states that the church is built on the foundation of apostles and prophets (see Eph. 2:20), we are wise to recognize their value and place in relation to the local church. Any builder knows you are foolish to build a great edifice on a faulty or nonexistent foundation. It will eventually sag and fall. Scripture plainly states that apostles and prophets are that foundation.

Now, I would not argue for a moment with anyone who points to that statement as a reference to the prophetically and apostolically originated Scriptures. The Holy Scripture certainly holds a unique place for us and serves as an apostolic blueprint for the building. I do, however, believe that apostolic and prophetic foundations also include present-day apostolic and prophetic people who themselves are foundational in the building, whose contribution serves to insure the blueprint is followed and proper foundations are laid for the kind of church God wants.

You may by now be realizing where I'm going with this analogy. How many faulty "buildings" do we have due to the lack of apostolic and prophetic input either resident within or fed translocally into local churches? Many of the existing "structures" were built on the foundation of a strong teaching ministry, or a strong evangelistic ministry, or even a strong pastoral ministry.

But if we want to experience a fully functioning New Testament church in the twenty-first century, we must fully embrace the entire five-fold leadership team of apostles, prophets, evangelists, pastors, and teachers. One of the vital issues of the church in this hour is how to properly build fully functioning team ministry and/or relate to translocal government within the body of Christ.

The church as a body has Jesus as the head. The relational focus of this picture is toward one another, toward our "connectedness," and toward our function.

> And He put all things under His feet, and gave Him to be head over all things to the church, which is His body, the fullness of Him who fills all in all (Ephesians 1:22-23).

> For as we have many members in one body, but all the members do not have the same function, so we, being many, are one body in Christ, and individually members of one another (Romans 12:4-5).

> For in fact the body is not one member but many. If the foot should say, "Because I am not a hand, I am not of the body," is it therefore

not of the body? And if the ear should say, "Because I am not an eye, I am not of the body," is it therefore not of the body? If the whole body were an eye, where would be the hearing? If the whole were hearing, where would be the smelling? But now God has set the members, each one of them, in the body just as He pleased. ... And the eye cannot say to the hand, "I have no need of you"; nor again the head to the feet, "I have no need of you." No, much rather, those members of the body which seem to be weaker are necessary. ... Now you are the body of Christ, and members individually. And God has appointed these in the church: first apostles, second prophets, third teachers, after that miracles, then gifts of healings, helps, administrations, varieties of tongues (1 Corinthians 12:14-18,21-22,27-28).

And He Himself gave some to be apostles, some prophets, some evangelists, and some pastors and teachers, for the equipping of the saints for the work of ministry, for the edifying of the body of Christ, till we all come to the unity of the faith and of the knowledge of the Son of God, to a perfect man, to the measure of the stature of the fullness of Christ; that we should no longer be children, tossed to and fro and carried about with every wind of doctrine, by the trickery of men, in the cunning craftiness of deceitful plotting, but, speaking the truth in love, may grow up in all things into Him who is the head—Christ— from whom the whole body, joined and knit together by what every joint supplies, according to the effective working by which every part does its share, causes growth of the body for the edifying of itself in love (Ephesians 4:11-16).

We know that God is raising up an entire generation of saints who will volunteer freely to do the work of the ministry in the day of His power. If the church is a body, every member is meant to have a function. No longer will the work be left to a few "professional" ministers, but rather, God wants a leadership who will be busy about the task of equipping the saints to do the work of the ministry. Most of the people I've known who want to de-emphasize "official leadership" in the church or somehow blur the demarcation between "leaders" and "members" seem to be doing so out of a commendable and valid motive to press the emphasis toward every member as a minister. God does want every member to be equipped, activated, and functioning. But if this is true, then someone needs to train them. Actually, we need both saints who will be ministers and leaders who will train them.

Now, let's look at another angle of this analogy and go back to the initial question of, "What is 'the church' and what isn't?" If we can belabor the body parts analogy as Paul does, let's think for a moment about what makes a living, viable body. There are quite a few functional body parts and a few vital body parts. God Himself put the fivefold ministry "body parts" in the body, and they are the vital organs.

This creates a series of questions for me: Can a body be missing body parts and still live? Will it be hindered in its ability to function, but still be a living body? Which body parts are valuable to have but not necessary for survival? Are there certain body parts within the body of Christ that are like vital organs that the body will swiftly die without? Can you pile a few arms, feet, and a leg or two together and call it a living body? Of course, a body can be missing a foot, and it will be handicapped but still live. However, a human body cannot survive without a heart or liver. Likewise, not every "pile" of body parts is the church.

Here is what we have begun to see. Not only has the eye said to the hand, "I have no need of you," but all kinds of body parts have been saying, "I have no need of you," to the very vital organs that God Himself has set in the body. The reality is that independence and isolation are sure signs of unhealthiness or immaturity. Proverbs 18:1 states, "A man who isolates himself seeks his own desire; he rages against all wise judgment." However, we are to grow up in all aspects into "...Christ—from whom the whole body, joined and knit together by what every joint supplies, according to the effective working by which every part does its share, causes growth of the body for the edifying of itself in love" (Eph. 4:15-16).

Let me become more specific. Having been part of the home cell movement for over 20 years, I have noted that cells that either have within them or are connected to fivefold ministry are vital organs. They are alive and fruitful. Those cells that are not so comprised or connected will either drift apart or degenerate into sick, introspective, unproductive cancer-like cells.

I also believe that as we see the culmination of the ages and the glorious church emerging, that it will be a church that is moving in apostolic power and structure, prophetic clarity, evangelistic fervor, pastoral care and nurture, and will be fed on insight and understanding from the teaching ministries in the church. It must be corporate, or it just won't become what God intended it to be.

Chapter 5

Apostles, Prophets, and Pastors

My first automobile had a strong V-8 engine in it. It had eight cylinders and a 409-cubic inch volume. That thing could roar down the road. In fact, I enjoyed gunning the engine so much, with that feeling of the power at my command, that eventually the drive shaft and rear end linkage fell out. That is a lot of torque.

The interesting thing about those eight-cylinder engines, however, was the fact that if a few of the spark plugs clogged, or for some reason some of the cylinders malfunctioned, there was enough torque coming out of the remaining cylinders to still keep the car moving. It would still go down the road, but it could not perform in the way that it was designed to. It was designed to work on all eight cylinders, but it was still nominally operational with just five or six cylinders working.

Such has been the status of the church for many years. God designed it to operate with a fivefold leadership engine. However, it has operated on two or three of its five cylinders for centuries. It has been able, at times, to have some forward momentum, but it simply has not had the full capacity to deliver the power that it could have and should have.

We need all five of the Lord's ascension gift ministries in operation to accomplish what God plans for the church at the end of the age. Since these ministries have not been operating as they should be, we are now in a time of rediscovering, redefining, and reimplementing them.

To the best of my ability, I have tried to arrive at the following definitions from the scriptural blueprint rather than from historical and traditional examples. I am dealing specifically with the ministries of apostle, prophet, and pastor as they directly relate to the "house" God is build-ing. This is not to deny the importance of the evangelist or teacher, for their contributions are also important. However, the functions of these respective ministries are outside the scope of this book. To define the fivefold ministries from the scriptural blueprint is in many cases easier to do with the newly re-emerging prophetic and apostolic ministries than with the more common ministry of pastor, since this ministry has often been modified by the church to make up the difference for the lack of having all five "cylinders" operating in the church. With that in mind, let us first look at the ministry of the apostle.

Jesus the Apostle

As with each of the ministry gifts, Jesus serves as our foremost model of the ministry of the apostle. Jesus alone was the full expression of the apostle, the prophet, the evangelist, the pastor/shepherd, and the teacher. When He ascended, His purpose for dividing up His ministry mantle into five parts is so that none could function alone and so that team ministry would be necessary to fully express the ministry of Jesus to the world. Hebrews 3 mentions the apostolic ministry of Jesus:

> *Therefore, holy brethren, partakers of the heavenly calling, consider the Apostle and High Priest of our confession, Christ Jesus, who was faithful to Him who appointed Him, as Moses also was faithful in all His house. For this One has been counted worthy of more glory than Moses, inasmuch as He who built the house has more honor than the house. For every house is built by someone, but He who built all things is God. And Moses indeed was faithful in all His house as a servant, for a testimony of those things which would be spoken afterward, but Christ as a Son over His own house, whose house we are if we hold fast the confidence and the rejoicing of the hope firm to the end* (Hebrews 3:1-6).

Jesus is called the Apostle and High Priest of our confession. We see that He was appointed as such from the Father, and He was sent to be a builder. The overall objective of the apostolic ministry is to reveal Jesus the Cornerstone and then to build something upon that revelation. Jesus said, "...I will build My church, and the gates of Hades shall not prevail against it" (Mt. 16:18). Jesus the Builder is Jesus the Apostle. Paul the apostle serves as a further model of the New Testament apostle, and his descriptions help us distinguish what other attributes of Jesus are part of His apostolic nature.

Who Is an Apostle?

Of course, in this day and hour, many are coming forth to proclaim themselves apostles. How can we know who is an apostle? Should we accept people's word for it if they come calling with the word *apostle* on their business card? Of course not! In fact, in the Book of Revelation the Lord commended the church in Ephesus for adequately distinguishing between those who were true and false apostles. Note the apostle John's words: "To the angel of the church of Ephesus write, ' ...I know your works, your labor, your patience, and that you cannot bear those who are evil. And you have tested those who say they are apostles and are not, and have found them liars' " (Rev. 2:1-2). We have the responsibility to discern between true and false apostles. The following are seven characteristics of a New Testament apostle. By them, we can know what an apostle is and does.

1. *Apostles have the grace upon their life to carry a revelation of Christ.* In Ephesians 3:5, Paul speaks of the mystery "which in other ages was not made known to the sons of men, as it has now been revealed by the Spirit to His holy apostles and prophets."

Paul realized the responsibility apostles and prophets have to reveal the "unsearchable riches of Christ" and the revelation of the mystery of the church (see Eph. 3:8-9). The purpose was "...that now the manifold wisdom of God might be made known by the church to the principalities and powers in the heavenly places" (Eph. 3:10).

It seems that there is a unique place that apostles and prophets have, in particular, to administrate the revelation of the mystery of Jesus, the One sent from God. Although there are many other aspects to the work of apostles and prophets, one function is primary, which is the ability to unfold the revelation of the unified corporate body called the church, including the greater revelation of the "unsearchable riches of Jesus" (who Jesus is and what He has done for mankind and all creation).

Stated more simply, the greatest purpose that the apostolic and prophetic ministries have—the ultimate goal above all else—is to bring a revelation of Jesus, to bring to light an unfolding of the unsearchable riches to be found in Jesus. It is to reveal the Cornerstone, who is Christ Jesus Himself!

2. *Apostles have the grace upon their life to carry a father/mentor anointing.* Paul told the Corinthian church, which he had planted, "For though you might have ten thousand instructors in Christ, yet you do not have many fathers; for in Christ Jesus I have begotten you through the gospel. Therefore I urge you, imitate me" (1 Cor. 4:15-16). He also instructed young apostle Timothy to be an equipper: "You therefore, my son, be

strong in the grace that is in Christ Jesus. And the things that you have heard from me among many witnesses, commit these to faithful men who will be able to teach others also" (2 Tim. 2:1-2).

Many of the apostolic ministries I have been exposed to simply have the feel of being a father. They will often have actually "begotten" and raised up sons in the faith, and they will have such a fatherly nurture, care, and steadfast heritage about them that causes those who are younger to want to be "adopted."

3. *Apostles have the grace upon their life to be team players, along with the ability to be team leaders.* Apostles realize that it takes a team. Although an apostle can sometimes seem to be a jack of all trades, he knows the overall objective can best be served through a team effort. Knowing the value of team and being able to accomplish it, however, are two different things. Part of the apostolic grace is that of being a Kingdom diplomat. An apostle can lead a team like no other. He is also able to command the respect of leaders who would be leadership material in their own right but who have also seen the higher good and greater accomplishment team effort will bring. A survey of the apostle Paul's ministry shows that he always traveled with a team. Jesus Himself instructed His apostles to go two by two. Two is the smallest team, but the more human resources are at the team leader's disposal, the better. If there are only two, however, the apostle and prophet should make every attempt to team up together, since there is a unique and foundation-setting dynamic that comes forth from the synergy created by the co-operation of these two ministries.

4. *Apostles have the grace upon their life to be general contractors for the building of God.* Paul called himself a master builder:

> *For we are God's fellow workers; you are God's field, you are God's building. According to the grace of God which was given to me, as a wise master builder I have laid the foundation, and another builds on it. But let each one take heed how he builds on it. For no other foundation can anyone lay than that which is laid, which is Jesus Christ. ... Do you not know that you are the temple of God and that the Spirit of God dwells in you?* (1 Corinthians 3:9-11,16)

The term *master builder* is actually *architekton* in the Greek language and is the root of our word *architect*, or in other words, a chief constructor or general contractor. A general contractor has the big picture. He knows what is to be built. Most of the general contractors I have known have a good general knowledge of the various specialized fields of the construction trade. They can do a little framing, electrical wiring, plumbing, roofing, etc., but that does not mean that they do it all. In fact, they will often bring in the specialists to do it, but they do know what they desire to see from the specialist and can also fill in, in a pinch.

It is the same with the apostle. Apostles whom I have observed have often filled many roles in their years of service before they emerged in an apostolic role. They are familiar with the overall "building project" of the Lord's church, knowing what needs to be done and when. They have the wisdom and the timing to call in the specialized ministries that will serve the purpose of the overall building project. Within this attribute is the ability to effectively plant churches and to see them brought forth to viable, local expressions of the body of Christ.

5. *Apostles have the grace upon their life to exercise governmental authority and dominion.* The essential meaning of the word *apostle* is "sent one." One very solid consequence of being sent by God is the authorization He gives. If you are sent by God, you have the very authority of God Himself backing you up. The restoration of apostolic ministry includes restoration to a whole new level of Kingdom dominion and authority, which is most evident through exercising dominion over the kingdom of darkness. However, it is also demonstrated by a new level of signs and wonders, including dominion over diseases and sickness. Luke 9:1-2 (NAS) states, "And He called the twelve together, and gave them power and authority over all the demons, and to heal diseases. And He sent them out to proclaim the kingdom of God, and to perform healing."

Demons recognize leaders whom God has authorized. As one preacher asked in the introduction and title to his message: "Are you known in hell?" This kind of spiritual authority is easily recognizable by those who are looking for it. Again, it was Paul who said to the Corinthian church, "But I will come to you shortly, if the Lord wills, and I will know, not the word of those who are puffed up, but the power. For the kingdom of God is not in word but in power" (1 Cor. 4:19-20). He was saying, in essence, "Talk is cheap, but let me see if you carry power."

That also includes the exercise of authority in the church. Of course, spiritual authority is not exercised in the same manner as the world does, but it is authority nonetheless. Those who know how authority works in the Kingdom of God and who recognize the grace of God's authority upon a person will wisely submit to it. David, a type of apostolic rulership for our age, did not foist his authority upon others; they simply recognized the leadership grace upon his life and were willing to follow.

6. *Apostles have the grace upon their life to demonstrate signs and wonders and to move in the supernatural.* Paul, when defending his calling as an apostle to the Corinthian church, stated: "Truly the signs of an apostle

were accomplished among you with all perseverance, in signs and wonders and mighty deeds" (2 Cor. 12:12).

Although the presence of signs and wonders cannot be the sole criteria for judging the credibility of a ministry, the absence of them certainly indicates a lack of God's supernatural endorsement. Paul's example is that he determined to minister more than just natural information but "...in demonstration of the Spirit and of power, that your faith should not be in the wisdom of men but in the power of God" (1 Cor. 2:4-5). He went on to say, "For the Kingdom of God does not consist in words, but in power" (1 Cor. 4:20 NAS).

In his next letter to the Corinthians he stated, "...but our sufficiency is from God, who also made us sufficient as ministers of the new covenant, not of the letter but of the Spirit; for the letter kills, but the Spirit gives life" (2 Cor. 3:5-6). God has called us to be ministers of the Spirit, to demonstrate the Spirit in power. The gifts and abilities of the Spirit are the supernatural "tools of the trade" for the building. We need His anointing to build His house.

7. *Apostles have the grace upon their life to bear fruit that remains, which they can point to as credible proof of their ministry.* Paul, when defending his apostleship, not only pointed to the endorsement of God through the witness of signs and wonders, but he also pointed to the simple fact that there were churches in existence as a result of his apostolic work. It was also to the Corinthians that he wrote, "Am I not an apostle?...If I am not an apostle to others, yet doubtless I am to you. For you are the seal of my apostleship in the Lord" (1 Cor. 9:1-2). Paul pointed out that there was a viable church in existence that proved he had the calling of an apostle.

Fruit that remains is the evidence of the calling and choosing of God upon a life. The Lord Jesus, in preparing His apostles for the great fruitfulness that was to come in their ministry, was careful to clarify one very important thing about their calling. He said, "You did not choose Me, but I chose you and appointed you that you should go and bear fruit, and that your fruit should remain..." (Jn. 15:16).

Someone may consider him or herself called to apostleship, but if there is no tangible fruit, that person is either mistaken or his ministry calling is in such an embryonic stage that he would do best to wait for the fruit to become manifest in his life before he calls himself an apostle. We can and should simply ask someone who is considering himself called as an apostle: "Where's the fruit? What have you built?"

Jesus the Prophet

As with the other fivefold ministry gifts described in Ephesians 4, the ministry of the New Testament prophet is a gift from the ascended Christ Jesus and proceeds out of what He was and is in Himself.

As with each of the ministry gifts, we must look to Jesus as our foremost model of the ministry of the prophet. The prophetic ministry Jesus had was described by Moses. The Lord told Moses, "I will raise up for them a Prophet like you from among their brethren, and will put My words in His mouth, and He shall speak to them all that I command Him" (Deut. 18:18).

Although the office was fully functioning throughout the Old Testament, it is important to see Jesus as our ultimate model of ministry because the task of the prophet is to communicate God's word with God's heart. And the fullest expression of God's heart is seen in the person of Jesus—not Elijah, not Jeremiah, not John the Baptist, but Jesus.

In fact, a story out of Luke's Gospel shows a very interesting contrast given by Jesus between Elijah's behavior and what He wanted His disciples to do in a situation that the disciples felt warranted "Elijah-type" behavior.

> *And [He] sent messengers before His face. And as they went, they entered a village of the Samaritans, to prepare for Him. But they did not receive Him, because His face was set for the journey to Jerusalem. And when His disciples James and John saw this, they said, "Lord, do You want us to command fire to come down from heaven and consume them, just as Elijah did?" But He turned and rebuked them, and said, "You do not know what manner of spirit you are of. For the Son of Man did not come to destroy men's lives but to save them." And they went to another village* (Luke 9:52-56).

We need to communicate the words of God out of the same spirit or attitude that God has.

Christ Jesus was and is that Prophet of whom Moses spoke.

> *For Moses truly said to the fathers, "The Lord your God will raise up for you a Prophet like me from your brethren. Him you shall hear in all things, whatever He says to you. And it shall be that every soul who will not hear that Prophet shall be utterly destroyed from among the people"* (Acts 3:22-23).

Therefore, Christ the Prophet gave prophets as gifts to the church to represent the prophetic aspect of His ministry.

The essence of prophetic ministry is to communicate God's words to the people. The obvious and necessary complement to that is to be able to perceive God's words, His heart, and His thoughts. Thus prophetic ministry is made up of gifts of perception and communication.

As we explore the various kinds of prophetic ministry in this chapter, we will find there are various expressions in the operation of the prophet. Before proceeding, however, I do want to clarify that the following is not meant to create a rigid definition or to promote one "kind" of prophet above another. We may err if we apply these definitions too rigidly.

Kinds of Prophets

One of the most confusing things I had to sort through as I began to look at the contemporary function of the office of prophet was that what was commonly called a prophet in certain circles was not at all what others would call a prophet. Some would point to very anointed preachers who carried a strong message to the church or to the contemporary culture and call them prophets. But, others would say, "Oh, but a prophet should be one who moves in the gift of prophecy." Some circles would relish yummy morsels of insight about the times, or some discernment about the body of Christ, and call that prophetic. Yet still others would point to persons who would simply open their mouth and gush forth some ecstatic utterance without giving it any cognitive thought at all.

My first personal exposure to a prophet was a man who mentored me for a time. His "burden" was the abortion issue. Although he was every bit a prophet, he certainly didn't look like what others commonly called prophets. He rarely "prophesied," but every time he preached you knew that you had just heard a fresh word from the "broken heart of God."

I then discovered John Sandford and his deep insights into the aspect of the prophet as a watchman, intercessor, and burden-bearer. Meanwhile, I was (and am) married to a woman who had no particular burden for the unborn, nor a strong inclination to intercessory burden-bearing, nor deep insights into the current body of Christ at large, but she could prophesy in an assembly or to individuals with such power and accuracy that it would make your hair stand on end. We eventually became affiliated with the ministry of Dr. Bill Hamon and the Christian International Network of Prophetic Ministries, a ministry dedicated to the equipping, activating, and releasing of prophets and believers into the gifting of prophecy.

What I have observed in the church at large in regard to this has been the forming of companies of prophets who seem to have gravitated to one another based on their particular dimension of the prophetic.

One potential problem with this, though, is that every "company" of prophets seems prone to having a hard time relating to and recognizing the value of the others.

A study of names given to prophets in Scripture reveals a spectrum of ministry, which varies within two primary components of the prophetic—perception and communication. Such a study reveals that there are various functions that are all prophetic according to Scripture and that are all valuable and necessary.

Seer or Watchman

In First Samuel 9:9, we find reference to the seer: "...when a man went to inquire of God, he spoke thus: 'Come, let us go to the seer'; for he who is now called a prophet was formerly called a seer." This word is *ro'eh* or *ra'ah*, and it refers to a person who sees—an observer, a person endowed with moral and spiritual insight or knowledge. Essentially, the root, *ro'eh*, means to look at or behold.

The seer is one who has understanding of the times. This person has the ability to perceive and discern the spiritual significance of a situation and can give the Lord's perspective on a given situation. This person's strengths are giftings of illumination and discernment, although they may or may not communicate what they see in one set or particular manner.

This kind of prophet is extremely valuable as a watchman and intercessor in the midst of the church. An interesting occurrence of this word in Scripture is found in Isaiah 21:8: "Then he cried, 'A lion [*ra'ah*], my Lord! I stand continually on the watchtower in the daytime; I have sat at my post every night." We see here the direct connection to the watchman ministry, and by implication, the ministry of spiritual warfare. A contemporary company of prophets, whom I would predominantly call seers, would be the MorningStar group that is led by Rick Joyner.

One of the observations I have made is that the manner of perceiving God's thoughts can be different with each individual, but it can be seen to follow or parallel our natural means of perception. That is, some "see," others "hear," while others "feel." For that matter, Scripture even indicates we can have a spiritual aroma (see 2 Cor. 2:15-16), or that we can "...taste and see that the Lord is good" (Ps. 34:8a). For instance, I find myself being a visual person, and often I will "see" pictures in my mind's eye. Other times, I will "feel" the heart of God concerning a matter. When prophetic inspiration comes in this way, I will know the "thought of God" and then labor to put words to the thoughts. When this is the case, I am often hesitant to express a "first person/as from the

Lord" kind of utterance. At other times, there is such an unction to prophesy that I can speak boldly as from the Lord.

Several of these forms of perception are listed in Numbers 12:6-8:

> *Then He said, "Hear now My words: If there is a prophet among you, I, the Lord, make Myself known to him in a vision; I speak to him in a dream. Not so with My servant Moses; he is faithful in all My house. I speak with him face to face, even plainly, and not in dark sayings; and he sees the form of the Lord. Why then were you not afraid to speak against My servant Moses?"*

Here we find reference to visions, dreams, dark sayings, and hearing God's words directly.

Contrary to me, my wife, Carolyn, is more of an auditory person. She has, in fact, "heard" the audible voice of God. She will often hear in her heart the exact words to be spoken and declare them as words from God.

Visionary

In First Chronicles 29:29, we find an occurrence of three different words, which refer to three different prophets: "Now the acts of King David, first and last, indeed they are written in the book of Samuel the seer [*ra'ah*], in the book of Nathan the prophet [*nabiy*], and in the book of Gad the seer [*chozeh*]." Although both Samuel and Gad were referred to as seers, the actual Hebrew word is different in the second case and carries some broader implications. The word is *chozeh* and is defined as a person of unusually keen foresight, a person who sees visions, or a beholder in vision. It is interesting that Asaph, David's musical prophet, was called a visionary. The primary root, *chazah*, means "to gaze at; mentally, to perceive, contemplate; specifically, to have a vision of." This kind of prophet is akin to the other seer, but the implications are that this person goes beyond simply seeing the current spiritual scenarios to having a vision of what God is going to do or wants to do.

A visionary has the unique ability to "envision" people to rally to the cause of the Kingdom. The Lord spoke to the prophet Habakkuk and said:

> *Write the vision, and make it plain upon tablets, that he may run that readeth it. For the vision is yet for the appointed time, and it hasteth toward the end, and shall not lie: though it tarry, wait for it; because it will surely come, it will not delay* (Habakkuk 2:2-3 ASV).

It is vision that motivates us to run. Proverbs 29:18a states, "Where there is no vision, the people perish" (KJV), or "cast off restraint" (NKJ).

In other words, vision motivates and controls our action. Without it, we wander aimlessly with no purpose or sit in apathy with no motivation. Vision gives us reason to redirect our actions into something productive. Vision is what moves us forward into the purposes of God.

An example of the envisioning work of the prophet is told in the story of Ezra, when the work came to a halt. Then arose the prophets Haggai and Zechariah. They were successful in stirring the people to arise and fulfill the vision. In the time of Ezra, the temple that had been torn down was in need of repair. The people had become apathetic toward the things of God and were content to live in a self-absorbed condition with no thought toward God's house. In the midst of this dilemma, the prophets arose and declared what God intended for His glorious temple. The people, then re-envisioned for the work, arose and built.

> So the elders of the Jews built, and they prospered through the prophesying of Haggai the prophet and Zechariah the son of Iddo. And they built and finished it, according to the commandment of the God of Israel, and according to the command of Cyrus, Darius, and Artaxerxes king of Persia (Ezra 6:14).

The Burden-Bearer

There are several places in Scripture where a prophetic message is called a "burden." For example, Isaiah 13:1 states, "The burden against Babylon which Isaiah the son of Amoz saw." This word *burden* speaks more to the function or message rather than the person, but should still be examined. Though the Hebrew word is *massa*, meaning simply "burden," it is used to describe prophetic utterances (see Prov. 31:1) and even prophetic musical dirges (see 1 Chron. 15:22). It implies the weightiness of the prophetic message that prophets are sometimes called to carry.

One of the first occurrences of the word *burden* used in conjunction with the prophetic ministry is in Numbers 11:16-17,24-25, where God placed Moses' prophetic mantle upon 70 elders:

> So the Lord said to Moses: "Gather to Me seventy men of the elders of Israel, whom you know to be the elders of the people and officers over them; bring them to the tabernacle of meeting, that they may stand there with you. Then I will come down and talk with you there. I will take of the Spirit that is upon you and will put the same upon them; and they shall bear the burden of the people with you, that you may not bear it yourself alone." ... So Moses went out and told the people the words of the Lord, and he gathered the seventy men of the elders of the people and placed them around the tabernacle. Then the Lord came down in the cloud, and spoke to him, and took of the Spirit that

was upon him, and placed the same upon the seventy elders; and it happened, when the Spirit rested upon them, that they prophesied....

The deeper implication of this as it pertains to the prophet is seen in the very first mention of a prophet in Scripture. Abraham is called a prophet in Genesis 20:7, where it says of him that, as he prayed, God would spare King Abimelech: "Now therefore, restore the man's wife; for he is a prophet, and he will pray for you and you shall live...."

Prophetic burden-bearers are called to pray. These are the prophetic intercessors. They can feel the grief of the Lord over the things that are not right. These prophets seem to live in the doldrums much of the time, but they are called there to pray "right" again those things that are wrong. God bless them!

The Herald

The last two kinds of prophets can be described by how they communicate more than how they receive communication from God. The *nataph,* or herald, is the prophetically inspired preacher. *Nataph* means, as a primary root word, to ooze; that is, distill gradually; by implication, to fall in drops; to let something soak in gradually, or figuratively, to speak by inspiration. The word is translated "preach" in Ezekiel 21:2: "Son of man, set your face toward Jerusalem, preach against the holy places, and prophesy against the land of Israel."

A herald is defined as "a royal or official messenger, particularly one representing a monarch in an ambassadorial capacity during wartime; a person or thing that proclaims or announces." To herald means to give tidings of, announce, proclaim, and publicize, to signal the coming of, to usher in.

One of the errors of the Pentecostal and Charismatic portions of the church has been to cast the prophet into the mold that says he or she must be one who exhibits the supernatural gift of the Holy Spirit to prophesy. Therefore, they will often neglect the prophetic voices of men such as Chuck Colson and others who are clearly prophetic voices to our generation. The content of their message is every bit prophetically inspired, and as their sermons or writings "soak in," you know you have heard from the heart of God on the matter. However, their mode of communication is not necessarily ecstatic utterance.

Oracle

The word *nabiy* is the most commonly used word in the Scripture for "prophet" and describes one who "gushes forth with an ecstatic utterance." This word describes one who functions as an oracle. The oracle is defined as "a person who delivers authoritative and usually influential

pronouncements; any utterance regarded as authoritative; a prophesi-
er." The root word is *naba'* and means "to speak or sing by inspiration."
A deeper connotation is "to bubble up, to gush forth, to pour forth."
This is the word used in Amos 3:8 (NIV), which states, "...The Sovereign
Lord has spoken—who can but prophesy [*naba'*]," and Joel 2:28, which
says, "...Your sons and your daughters shall prophesy [*naba'*]."

This is the "ecstatic prophetic utterance" prophet who speaks forth
in the name of the Lord with a confident, "Thus says the Lord...." This
particular ministry goes beyond simple inspired insight, beyond prophetically insightful preaching or writing, and actually speaks God's words
into a situation. Prophet Bill Hamon gives a simple and direct definition
of this manner of prophetic ministry; he simply defines it as "God talking." This kind of ministry may often utilize any of the various manners
through which we perceive what God has to say and then, with a vocal
gifting, will speak it forth with power. Although there are differing opinions across the body of Christ about direct, "first person" prophesying,
it is very clearly the most common mode of prophetic ministry throughout the Bible.

The Gift of Prophecy

The oracle moves in the gift of prophecy. The *naba'* prophet speaks
forth what God is saying to the church, individual, or situation through
a vocal gifting from the Holy Spirit (see 1 Cor. 12–14). Often, it is as if
these words just "bubble up" or gush forth from within the spirit, sometimes with barely any forethought. Although other kinds of prophets
may or may not move in the supernatural "ecstatic utterance" gift of
prophecy, the oracle clearly does.

Regarding this gift of prophecy, a close examination of the instructions in the above Scriptures clearly shows that not all are prophets, but
on the other hand, all may prophesy. In fact, we are to earnestly desire
to prophesy (see 1 Cor. 12:31; 14:1). Herein is also one of the biggest
confusions about the office of prophet. We surely cannot turn everyone
into prophets, but if the prophets are doing their "equipping" job as
described in Ephesians 4, they will be stirring up the prophetic gifting
within the members of the church. We can make it a valid and worthy
goal to equip as many as possible to prophesy.

Pastors

Much of the church structure of the twentieth century is an old
wineskin that cannot contain the wine that God is going to pour out for
a final harvest at the end of the age. One of the major changes that must
take place is the redefining of the role of leaders, as we see a full fivefold

ministry model being restored. Although we are excited about the emergence of apostolic and prophetic ministries in these days, it is also essential to note that the ministry of "pastor" has evolved through tradition into something quite different than the scriptural definition and needs redefining as well. For instance, nowhere in the New Testament do we find a pastor being the solo minister of a local church. What we do see is churches led by apostles over teams of ministers, some of which were prophets, pastors, teachers, evangelists, administrators, and many under the general catchall grouping of "elders." We see, for instance, in the case of the Antioch church from which Paul's apostolic team was sent, certain prophets and teachers giving leadership to the church. The common government of the New Testament church was a plurality of elders, made up of a diversity of offices and giftings, who recognized within their midst headship, diversity of gifting, apostolic grace to lead, and prophetic grace to cast forth the vision.

Am I saying that the church does not need pastors and pastoral leaders? On the contrary, the church needs pastoral ministry more than ever. But let's define biblical pastoral ministry, and we will discover a few things that will change our perspective of exactly what a pastor is. It is my strong opinion that an effective church needs a whole team of pastors to effectively "pastor" a church.

We first look to the job description found in Ezekiel 34 that makes most present-day pastors cringe.

> *And the word of the Lord came to me, saying, "Son of man, prophesy against the shepherds of Israel, prophesy and say to them, 'Thus says the Lord God to the shepherds: "Woe to the shepherds of Israel who feed themselves! Should not the shepherds feed the flocks? You eat the fat and clothe yourselves with the wool; you slaughter the fatlings, but you do not feed the flock. The weak you have not strengthened, nor have you healed those who were sick, nor bound up the broken, nor brought back what was driven away, nor sought what was lost; but with force and cruelty you have ruled them." ' " ... " 'For thus says the Lord God: "Indeed I Myself will search for My sheep and seek them out. As a shepherd seeks out his flock on the day he is among his scattered sheep, so will I seek out My sheep and deliver them from all the places where they were scattered on a cloudy and dark day. ... I will feed My flock, and I will make them lie down," says the Lord God. "I will seek what was lost and bring back what was driven away, bind up the broken and strengthen what was sick; but I will destroy the fat and the strong, and feed them in judgment" ' " (Ezekiel 34:1-4, 11-12,15-16).*

We see here that the Lord rebuked the shepherds who failed to feed the flock, strengthen them, gather them, heal them, bind up the broken, and protect them from harm. It is the description of one who protects, corrects, guides, and provides. In essence, this can be described as the "ministry of feeding and caring" as expressed in these tangible ways.

A pastor will feed the people with knowledge and understanding from an anointing to teach and impart biblical truth. But he will also bear the people in his heart, pray for healing when they are hurting and sick, tend to their souls, and will round them up when they are drifting away. A pastor is the expression of the individual care that Jesus has for His flock. We see the promise of a shepherd in Jeremiah 3:14-15:

> *"Return, O backsliding children," says the Lord; "for I am married to you. I will take you, one from a city and two from a family, and I will bring you to Zion. And I will give you shepherds according to My heart, who will feed you with knowledge and understanding."*

With a job description as the Bible gives, it is my opinion that it is only realistic to expect a pastor to effectively "shepherd" somewhere around 50 to 80 people. It is interesting to note the fact that the average sized church in North America is between 60 to 80 people. So what we have is many churches built on pastoral foundations rather than apostolic/prophetic ones, which grow to about 50 to 75 people and plateau. To do the job effectively, it takes a team.

"But," you might ask, "what of the few very large churches that are led by pastors?" The very simple answer is that there are a number of churches built on the anointing and gifting of an apostle who is being called "pastor," teaching ministries who are calling themselves "pastors," or prophets who are being called "pastors." Even evangelists can gather multitudes and, while not pastoring them, be called "pastors."

For the typical local church, that means several things regarding the ministry of the pastor. It means they need a willingness to recognize and make a place for a new wineskin of leadership and ministry. In many cases it will take a whole new structuring of the government of the church to make room for apostolic and prophetic foundation layers to work. Some wineskins will be flexible, some will not. It also means that we must simplify the description of "pastoring" so as to recognize that many can participate in the ministry of feeding and caring. It also means that we must begin to recognize the many "pastoral" people in our midst that God has gifted to "pastor" the people.

Section III

The Foundation Secured

Do two walk together unless they have agreed to do so? (Amos 3:3 NIV)

...the whole building, being fitted together is growing into a holy temple in the Lord (Ephesians 2:21 NAS).

Chapter 6

Relationship: The Mortar Between the Bricks

The Importance of Relationships

Two are better than one, because they have a good reward for their labor. For if they fall, one will lift up his companion. But woe to him who is alone when he falls, for he has no one to help him up (Ecclesiastes 4:9-10).

As iron sharpens iron, so a man sharpens the countenance of his friend (Proverbs 27:17).

Consequently, you are no longer foreigners and aliens, but fellow citizens with God's people and members of God's household, built on the foundation of the apostles and prophets, with Christ Jesus Himself as the chief cornerstone. In Him the whole building is joined together and rises to become a holy temple in the Lord. And in Him you too are being built together to become a dwelling in which God lives by His Spirit (Ephesians 2:19-22 NIV).

God designed and intended for us to be in relationship. In fact, the only thing He claimed was "not good" in His creation as told in Genesis 1–2 was for man to be alone. This is why He created a partner for man (see Gen. 2:18). God designed us to be relational beings. He made us in His image, and He Himself is a relational being. We (humanity), through the fall of man, have had our vital relationships broken and damaged.

An important part of God's agenda is to bring us back into wholeness relationally.

In fact, an integral part of God's healing and redemption of mankind from our fall into sin is a restoration of true and proper relationship with God and with one another. Scripture tells us a lot about how we should relate to one another. In fact, the fruit of the Spirit predominately centers around relational issues, demonstrating that God wants to assist us in rightly relating to one another.

Seven "One Anothers" in Scripture

The following are just seven of the many important directives from Scripture about how we should relate to one another and what we should do for one another.

Love One Another

> *A new commandment I give to you, that you love one another; as I have loved you, that you also love one another. By this all will know that you are My disciples, if you have love for one another* (John 13:34-35).

> *For this is the message that you heard from the beginning, that we should love one another* (1 John 3:11).

Restore One Another

> *Brethren, if a man is overtaken in any trespass, you who are spiritual restore such a one in a spirit of gentleness, considering yourself lest you also be tempted. Bear one another's burdens, and so fulfill the law of Christ* (Galatians 6:1-2).

Bear With and Forgive One Another

> *Therefore, as the elect of God, holy and beloved, put on tender mercies, kindness, humility, meekness, longsuffering; bearing with one another, and forgiving one another, if anyone has a complaint against another; even as Christ forgave you, so you also must do* (Colossians 3:12-13).

Build Up One Another

> *Therefore encourage one another, and build up one another, just as you also are doing* (1 Thessalonians 5:11 NAS).

Encourage to Believe and Protect From Deception

> *Beware, brethren, lest there be in any of you an evil heart of unbelief in departing from the living God; but exhort one another daily, while*

it is called "Today," lest any of you be hardened through the deceit-
fulness of sin (Hebrews 3:12-13).

Stir One Another to Love and Good Works and Encourage Hope

And let us consider one another in order to stir up love and good
works, not forsaking the assembling of ourselves together, as is the
manner of some, but exhorting one another, and so much the more as
you see the Day approaching (Hebrews 10:24-25).

Confess Faults to One Another for Prayer and Healing

Confess your trespasses to one another, and pray for one another, that
you may be healed. The effective, fervent prayer of a righteous man
avails much (James 5:16).

First Things First

Relationships are important. However, when talking about relationships, it is vital that we place all our relationships into the right order
of priority. Even relationships can become idolatrous if we place them
above our relationship with God.

The following is a list of relationships in order of the priority they
should have in our lives.

1. God—Our first need is to come back into right relationship with
God, to be restored into relationship with Him. God was indwelt in
Christ, calling the world back to reconciliation with Himself.

2. Self—We need to come back into right relationship with ourselves. The fact is, there is a war within our members, the flesh against
the Spirit, and God wants us to come into peace within ourselves through
surrender to Him. Are you at peace with yourself? Only out of peace with
God can you truly make peace with yourself (gaining victory in issues
such as guilt, priorities, purpose, ambitions, self-hate, self-rejection, etc.).

3. Family (or our immediate significant others)—Love and cherish
your spouse as you do yourself.

So husbands ought to love their own wives as their own bodies; he who
loves his wife loves himself. For no one ever hated his own flesh, but
nourishes and cherishes it, just as the Lord does the church. For we
are members of His body, of His flesh and of His bones (Ephesians
5:28-30).

Manage your own household well.

One who rules his own house well, having his children in submis-
sion with all reverence (for if a man does not know how to rule his

own house, how will he take care of the church of God?) (1 Timothy 3:4-5)

4. The household of faith—Have a right relationship with the body of Christ.

Consequently, you are no longer foreigners and aliens, but fellow citizens with God's people and members of God's household, built on the foundation of the apostles and prophets, with Christ Jesus Himself as the chief cornerstone. In Him the whole building is joined together and rises to become a holy temple in the Lord. And in Him you too are being built together to become a dwelling in which God lives by His Spirit (Ephesians 2:19-22 NIV).

Therefore, as we have opportunity, let us do good to all, especially to those who are of the household of faith (Galatians 6:10).

5. The World—Jerusalem, Judea, Samaria, and the uttermost parts of the earth (see Acts 1:8). These were the last directives of Jesus:

And Jesus came and spoke to them, saying, "All authority has been given to Me in heaven and on earth. Go therefore and make disciples of all the nations, baptizing them in the name of the Father and of the Son and of the Holy Spirit, teaching them to observe all things that I have commanded you; and lo, I am with you always, even to the end of the age." Amen (Matthew 28:18-20).

No one is fully equipped to survive, much less thrive, by themselves. Our own weaknesses, blind spots, limited capabilities, and lack of experience point to one thing—interdependence. In fact, it is in relationship and fellowship that we find a release of God's life in our midst. Fellowship is a part of God's very nature, and it is a source of life for us.

In the beginning was the Word, and the Word was with God, and the Word was God. He was in the beginning with God. All things were made through Him, and without Him nothing was made that was made. In Him was life, and the life was the light of men (John 1:1-4).

This short section of Scripture gives us incredible insight into the nature and preexistence of our Creator before the beginning of time. There are some important insights we can gain from this Scripture as we look at it closely.

Here we see one of the most obvious declarations of the deity of Jesus as the preincarnate Word, preexistent with the Father and yet, later, manifest in the flesh as declared in the following verse:

And the Word became flesh and dwelt among us, and we beheld His glory, the glory as of the only begotten of the Father, full of grace and truth (John 1:14).

But one of the most exciting realities comes from a deeper look at the phrase in John 1:1, "And the Word was with God." This simple word *with* takes on a much deeper significance when looked at in the original language. The word is *pros*, literally meaning "to" or "toward." So Jesus and the Father were "to" or "toward" one another throughout eternity past, even before the creation of the existing universe.

So what does that mean? It means that the Trinity of God—Father, Son, and Holy Spirit—was in the delight of eternal fellowship before time began. In other words, God, by His very nature, is a fellowshiping God. He delights in fellowshiping within Himself and wants to fellowship with us as well.

We see how much God delighted in His Son from Scriptures where He is called "the Son of His love" (Col. 1:13) and "My beloved Son, in whom I am well pleased" (Mt. 3:17). So we see that God, by His very nature, is a fellowshiping God. Throughout eternity He has delighted in "fellowshiping" within His triune Self and now wants to include us in the fellowship that the Father has with the Son. It is most amazing how much He also wants that same fellowship with us as His creation. Jesus prayed in John 17:21, "That they all may be one, as You, Father, are in Me, and I in You; that they also may be one in Us...."

The apostle carried this theme into his Epistle of First John where he says, "That which we have seen and heard we declare to you, that you also may have fellowship with us; and truly our fellowship is with the Father and with His Son Jesus Christ" (1:3). Jesus Himself said it again in Revelation 3:20, "Behold I stand at the door and knock. If anyone hears My voice and opens the door, I will come into him and dine [commune, fellowship] with him, and he with Me."

Now let's look at some other parts of Jesus' prayer in John 17:

And this is eternal life, that they may know You, the only true God, and Jesus Christ whom You have sent. ... And the glory which You gave Me I have given them, that they may be one just as We are one (John 17:3,22).

I believe God delights in fellowshiping with us more than we would ever know. Furthermore, it is in the midst of the beauty and delight of this fellowship with God, that we find the true source of life. "In Him was life, and the life was the light of men" (Jn. 1:4). It is here that we find fullness of joy and love that is eternal. It is in the process of loving and fellowshiping with God that we find life springing up afresh in our souls.

The place of fellowship is the place of life. But God has called us not only into fellowship with Him, but also into fellowship with one another. And in as much as we experience fresh life through fellowship in His Spirit, we share that life to others as we enjoy our fellowship with one another.

It is important to understand that the source of our unity and fellowship is in Him. Jesus prayed to the Father, "I in them, and You in Me; that they may be made perfect in one..." (Jn. 17:23). This implies we can participate in the life of Jesus as He participates in the life of His Father. We can experience union with the life and eternal glory of Jesus as He is united with the life and glory of His Father. That is, Jesus abides in us as the Father abides in Him, and we experience fellowship with Jesus to the same degree that He has fellowshiped with the Father throughout eternity. But then, that is also the nature of our unity and fellowship with one another. When we think of joyful, loving, life producing, abundant fellowship with God, that is also what He wants us to, in turn, experience with one another.

Jesus gave this commandment: "...that you love one another; as I have loved you, that you also love one another" (Jn.13:34). He also said, "...inasmuch as you did it to one of the least of these My brethren, you did it to Me" (Mt. 25:40).

As we love one another, we love Him. As we enjoy one another, we enjoy Him. In caring for each other, we care for Him. In opening our hearts and lives to one another, we invite His presence. In pouring our lives out for one another, we pour out our expression of His love back to Him.

Jesus dwells in His church, and He expresses Himself through His church. As we fellowship with each other, we quietly and almost unnoticeably come in contact with Him. Just as we have entered into fellowship with Him, we continue to experience Him and spread the experience of Him to our other brothers and sisters in Christ. "...If we love one another, God abides in us, and His love has been perfected in us" (1 Jn. 4:12).

The Hurdle of Corporateness

God insists that we be rightly related to one another. The Scriptures in First John 2:9-11 and 3:19-21 imply that if we want to stay in right relationship with God, we must be about the work of maintaining a right relationship with our brothers and sisters in Christ. This means that the task of building and maintaining right relationships is not an optional sideline, but rather, it is an essential ingredient of our Christian life.

In Ephesians 2:19-21, Paul the apostle states that we are no longer alienated, but rather fellow citizens with the saints. We are being "fitted together" and "built together" into a dwelling of God. God wants us to be connected by relationship with one another.

Independence and isolation are sure signs of unhealthiness or immaturity. Proverbs 18:1 (NAS) states, "He who separates himself seeks his own desire, he quarrels against all sound wisdom." Instead we are to "grow up in all aspects into...Christ, from whom the whole body, being fitted and held together by that which every joint supplies, according to the proper working of each individual part, causes the growth of the body for the building up of itself in love" (Eph. 4:15-16 NAS).

As I mentioned before, God cares so much about our relating to one another in the right way that He has intertwined the way He relates to us with how we relate to each other. Mark 11 holds the most prevalent example, where God stated that if we do not forgive others, He will not forgive us. Also, Jesus said that all of the law was summarized as our loving God and loving one another (see Mt. 22:37-40).

Being rightly related also speaks to the issue of proper structure and government within the church. Being rightly fitted and held together includes understanding how to relate to spiritual authority and how to properly exercise spiritual authority, a touchy issue to be sure, but one that faces us all. It also means more than experiencing healthy relationships and proper structure within; it is also having proper relationship with the greater body of Christ.

Proper relationship with the larger body of Christ necessitates recognizing both peer relationships and mentor relationships. Peer relationships with other ministries are those in which we form alliances and coalitions for more effective ministry. Mentor relationships are those in which we receive instruction, oversight, and accountability. Since Scripture states that the church is built on the foundation of apostles and prophets (see Eph. 2:20) and since these ministries are more often translocal in nature rather than within the local church, we are wise to recognize their value and place in relation to the local church.

Every local church must always recognize the need to network with the larger body of Christ. Psalms 133 states that where the brethren dwell together in unity, there the Lord commands a blessing. We must always recognize that we are only a part of God's work in our city. These relationships are vital to the ongoing health of any church or ministry. One of the vital issues of the church in the years to come is destined to be how to properly relate to translocal government within the body of Christ.

God desires to bring into the body of Christ a level of unity and team ministry that is significantly lacking right now. We need to recognize our need for one another. We need to recognize our need for foundational input from apostles and prophets. These gifts are given to us by our ascended Lord and Savior Jesus because He thinks we need them. I agree with Him.

In a chapter called "The Kingdom Net," from his ground-breaking book called *Apostles and the Emerging Apostolic Movement,*[1] Dr. David Cannistraci builds on the concept found in Ephesians 4:16 (NAS): "From whom the whole body, being fitted and held together by that which every joint supplies, according to the proper working of each individual part, causes the growth of the body for the building up of itself in love."

He states that the trend away from denominationalism is giving way instead to things, such as alliances and networks. Networks and alliances work from the basis of relationship rather than organizational structure. The body of Christ is "joined together and united" through relationship. The key and operative word here is *relationship*. He states, "True apostles are people who are willing to merge their gifts with the gifts of others in the Body of Christ to properly establish the Kingdom. Apostles and prophets have a unique blending of gifts and often work together in this regard."

I would add, one of the most obvious indicators of a true apostle (although certainly not the only one) is the grace upon his life to relate well to others. (And we all know how much work relationships can sometimes be.)

However, the historic trend has always been that the most recent previous restoration "movement" is the one who is tested the most when the next thing comes from God. There are always some who make the transition into the next thing, and others who stumble for some reason or other and don't make the turn.

We have seen the rise of the prophets over the last two decades of this century. Praise God for that! During that time, we also saw that there were some teaching ministries and pastoral ministries of the 1970's and 80's that had a hard time embracing the prophetic ministries in the 90's. This is not surprising, since every restoration movement presents things that require adjustment for the rest of the church. The prophets have

---

1.   *Apostles and the Emerging Apostolic Movement* (formerly, *The Gift of the Apostle*) (Ventura, CA: Regal Books, 1996).

been established with all the fringes and abuses that any fresh movement has, but at least they are here.

I have been very intrigued to watch a trend that Dr. Bill Hamon describes very adeptly in his book, *Prophets and the Prophetic Movement*. He says that throughout history each restorational movement seems to be most adamantly resisted by the most recent prior movement. He showed how this happened over and over again all the way to the current century. If the trend continues, the implications are that many of the prophets who have emerged and found recognition during the previous ten years of the "prophetic movement" are in danger of being the very ones who will most strongly resist the "apostolic movement."

The apostolic movement is coming forth. There are some important questions to ask, such as "What elements does it contain that require adjustment?" and "Which ones will require the prophets particularly (as the most recent previous restorational move) to adjust to?" Although the rising of prophets required men and women to rise up and speak for God with no regard for anyone's differing opinion, that itself can be driven out of bounds if not brought into certain accountability and limits. Some of these limits are the emergence of "proper" government and accountability within the body of Christ—one of the specific characteristics of the emerging apostolic movement.

What God needs are prophets who are courageous enough to stand alone when they need to but who are also wise and humble enough to recognize their need of corporateness. God needs prophets who can embrace submission to authority and become co-laborers with apostles so that together they will be foundational to the church that God wants to build. In the 1970's, independence was the virtue. Now, the ability to be corporate is the valuable virtue. Some will make the turn; some will not.

The prophets who cannot or will not transition into team ministry will be the ones who become the enemies of this emerging restorational movement. Prophets who will not receive the grace from God to become corporate will find themselves sliding into delusion and error. We were designed by God for relationship and for interdependence. We are not called to an unhealthy dependence (born out of fear of man, people pleasing, and fear of rejection), nor independence (born out of pride and rebellion), but interdependence—having the courage to stand alone, but also, the humility to recognize our need for one another.

One of the tests for the prophets during this new season in God's restoration purposes will be the ability to remain teachable, accountable, and therefore, of greater usefulness for the larger good of the church.

Team ministry will always produce exponentially more progress than any solo ministry. Many of the kinds of things that God winked at within the prophetic movement in the past are now being challenged. This particularly includes the anti-relational elements. Relationships take love. Relationships take humility. Relationships take work.

Another test for the prophets is whether they can embrace a "builder" mentality that is a driving motive in the heart of the apostolic. Anyone can tear down. God wants something to be built. Anyone can be an "accuser of the brethren," but God wants an intercessor for the brethren. Many prophets like to embrace the first half of Jeremiah's call "to root out and to pull down, to destroy and to throw down," not realizing they also need to do the second half, "to build and to plant" (see Jer. 1:10b).

It is essential to realize that God designed for there to be a unique relationship and placement between the apostle and prophet. The church has the interesting description of being built upon the foundation of apostles and prophets together (see Eph. 2:20). A church without both foundational influences will be crippled and not all that God intends for it to be. In fact, what we've seen most often instead is a church built upon the work of an evangelist, a pastor, or even a teaching ministry; but when we see the final version, it will be something much more glorious.

The church needs apostles and prophets, and apostles and prophets need each other. It seems that the apostle is more often characterized by gifts of power and signs, while the prophet more often functions in the revelatory gifts. The prophet receives supernatural revelation; the apostle, supernatural wisdom. The prophet "sees" what and when to build; the apostle "knows how" to build it. When left alone, the apostle will build wonderful but sterile structures. The prophet left alone will have everyone so envisioned and motivated that they burn out before they can build anything that has permanence; otherwise, in his zeal for the pure and perfected church, he will continue to pull down and rip apart anything that is less.

It is obvious that God knew just what kind of tension and balance was needed in the building of the church. He told us that apostles and prophets together form the foundation for His church. When apostles and prophets find the grace to embrace each others' distinctive gifts and roles and work together, you have a wonderful foundation upon which something of worth to the Kingdom of God can be built—with Jesus, of course, as the Cornerstone.

Chapter 7

The Integrity of the Building Blocks

For it is the God who commanded light to shine out of darkness, who has shone in our hearts to give the light of the knowledge of the glory of God in the face of Jesus Christ. But we have this treasure in earthen vessels, that the excellence of the power may be of God and not of us (2 Corinthians 4:6-7).

A foundational leader is a unique instrument in the hand of God. He/she is prepared by God to communicate the knowledge of the glory of God to humanity. We do, however, have this problem of a wonderful treasure in earthen vessels. Although there is an adequate provision through the cross of Christ to render our flesh dead indeed unto sin, the working out of that great positional truth is, in reality, a lifelong process. The apostle Paul even admitted God had to allow a messenger from satan in the form of some kind of "thorn in the flesh" to buffet him lest he be lifted up in pride over the level of revelation given to him (see 2 Cor. 12:7). There often seems to remain just enough of a residue of self in us to keep us recognizing that the excellency of the power is of God and not of us.

Character Versus Gifting

It is also important to realize there is a very distinct difference between gifting and character. The reality is, gifting does not ensure character. Much of my life I have had a running dialog with God about how He seems, at times, to give away giftings to unscrupulous characters.

(Of course, He's been known to even use donkeys when needed.) The fact is, giftings are received by faith. Character is grown as fruit. The one does not ensure the other. Anointing *does not* automatically guarantee a person's correct doctrine, character, or maturity level. This is a very, very important lesson to learn, especially in this day when we are seeing a resurgence of many signs and wonders and supernatural giftings, making it critical that the church move in wisdom and discernment.

The sad lesson that we see from biblical, as well as contemporary examples, is that gifting without character and maturity can actually contribute to a minister's demise. We see King Saul, for example, who was a very gifted and charismatic leader, but whose lack of a foundation of character eventually caught up to him. Or we see Jonah, a prophet who had a severe unforgiveness problem, and though his ministry was very successful to the people of Nineveh, it only led him to suicidal depression. (A more thorough dealing with this story can be found in Chapter 9 of this book, where I take an in-depth look at Jonah and the problem of angry prophets.)

With that concept in mind, we can understand that God will demonstrate His wisdom and love through the "processes" He takes His leaders through as He prepares them for greater usefulness. It is not pleasant, but it is necessary. Hebrews 12:11 (NAS) states, "All discipline for the moment seems not to be joyful, but sorrowful; yet to those who have been trained by it, afterwards it yields the peaceful fruit of righteousness." It is with loving care that God goes about beating the "self life" out of us so that we can be mightily used by Him. One man put it very well when he said that "death to self" is like the insulation on an electrical wire so that God can pour His voltage through it without it damaging everything with which the wire comes in contact. If we have selfish motives intact, we become dangerous when the "juice" starts flowing.

We also need to see that God deals with a man or woman in terms of their entire lifetime, as they invite Him to move them slowly but surely toward their destiny. He seems at times to not be in a hurry at all. Then, at other times, He takes us on a crash course to learn some hard but necessary lessons. He does all this with our good as well as our usefulness in mind.

Preparation and Release

One thing I love about the Lord is that He refuses to be put into a box. Additional insight on this topic can be seen from the aspect of the calling and preparation of Jeremiah.

The Lord told Jeremiah, "Before I formed you in the womb I knew you; before you were born I sanctified you; I ordained you a prophet to the nations" (Jer. 1:5). This gives an additional dimension to the topic of "calling, preparation, and placement." God was preparing Jeremiah before he even entered this world!

This brings up the whole issue of God's pre-ordained purpose and destiny for each one of us. It seems that God begins to form us and put into us the raw ingredients that we need to be what He has planned and purposed us to be from the beginning of our life.

You cannot, of course, turn yourself into a prophet just by wanting to be one if God hasn't purposed it. But you can cooperate with His plans for you through the pursuit of your calling, as Paul said in Philippians 3:14: "I press toward the goal for the prize of the upward call of God in Christ Jesus." You frustrate His destiny in your life by dragging your feet through sin and rebellion.

God is at work in us, forming us and training us, sometimes before we even know what He is up to. He is laying the foundations in us so that when the time comes for the anointing to come upon us, we are adequate to do the job for which He has called and commissioned us.

A very intriguing story related to this has to do with King Saul at the time he was coming into his kingship. In First Samuel, we see Samuel instructing Saul with the following:

> *"Then the Spirit of the Lord will come upon you, and you will prophesy with them and be turned into another man." ... So it was, when he had turned his back to go from Samuel, that God gave him another heart; and all those signs came to pass that day. When they came there to the hill, there was a group of prophets to meet him; then the Spirit of God came upon him, and he prophesied among them. And it happened, when all who knew him formerly saw that he indeed prophesied among the prophets, that the people said to one another, "What is this that has come upon the son of Kish? Is Saul also among the prophets?" ...Therefore it became a proverb: "Is Saul also among the prophets?"* (1 Samuel 10:6,9-12)

This story exemplifies the reality that there can be a transference of anointing by entering into the "company of prophets." There can come a point in time when giftings are imparted and we are changed. Many of the renewal/revival centers around the globe at this time are also demonstrating this principle. There is such a thing as an anointing from God that can be transferred and imparted to others. I will repeat, however, *"This does not ensure character!"* Saul's insecurity and character flaws are what destroyed him in the end.

David serves as an example, on the other hand, of someone who was anointed by Samuel and functioned in his "prophetic-ness" for over 20 years before finally coming into his ultimate placement. We can also easily see the grueling processes David endured in preparation for his kingship.

In my own case, I caught glimpses of the fact that God had a call upon my life even as a youngster. Then for several years others would tell me that I was prophetic, but I had a hard time believing it because the gifting would only come in occasional spurts. Later came the time when I associated myself with a company of prophets. Hands were laid on me, and it was as if booster rockets were put on my back and my ministry went into orbit. I then began to see the wisdom in God's previous painstaking character curriculum through the processes of my life.

My wife, Carolyn, is also an example of how God can be at work in a life ahead of time. For instance, she took speech classes in school and actually won first place awards for public speaking in high school. Then, the night she surrendered her life to the Lord at age 19, it was prophesied to her that she would be prophesying within three months. She didn't even know what prophecy was at the time, but within three months she was doing it.

Her gifting also developed over a number of years through regular use (see Heb. 5:14). Then when we associated with a group of prophets 11 years later, her gifting went to even deeper dimensions of anointing and ability.

I've also seen in my own ministry times when I could lay hands on someone and a fresh anointing was imparted. It was as if the dry kindling that God had put there was suddenly ignited and began to blaze. This is why God says not to lay hands hastily on anyone (see 1 Tim. 5:22). That is, we should not bless, commission, or ordain someone prior to a great measure of character being worked into their life.

I've often heard Dr. Bill Hamon repeat a statement regarding ordinations, indicating that he does not believe in laying empty hands on empty heads. He means that someone with the "goods" can impart anointing and gifting to someone else who has done their "homework" of proper preparation for ministry. The giftings and anointing imparted may then be preserved within the container of character and integrity.

So, my conclusion is that there is a work God does throughout our lives to prepare us for our destiny and purpose. There is also an anointing that can come to us through association, mentoring, and transference through the laying on of hands that moves us forward in our ability to do the work He calls us to do.

Even if we receive certain giftings and we can master the skill of "message giving," the Holy Spirit has an agenda to make the messenger as well as the message. It is interesting to note that Balaam, whose story is in the Book of Numbers, delivered very accurate prophetic words and even gave the only Messianic prophecy recorded in the Book of Numbers, yet he was called a false prophet in the New Testament. Why? It was a character issue. God goes about making the messenger as well as giving him the message.

God has an utmost interest in the character issue. I once heard prophet John Sandford say that he has observed God intentionally allowing a prophet to "miss it" on occasion just to keep the prophet from getting too puffed up in his own sense of infallibility (ouch). I have come to believe through my own observations that any prophetic minister who claims infallibility has already deluded himself and is a very dangerous person. I'll go even further to say that I have also observed many well-intended Christians who have felt they could hear God for themselves to such an extent they had no need of anyone else to speak into their lives. Invariably these individuals ended in deception. Although we certainly can and should hear God for ourselves, God also wants us ever mindful of our need for one another.

It is good to recognize that the communications we receive in our "spirit man" are still filtered through our own personality and character. Watchman Nee brings this incredible concept out in his book, *The Ministry of God's Word*, where he showed that even Holy Scripture—every jot and tittle of which is God-inspired—still has the flavor of the particular author (e.g., Paul's style of writing versus John's style), yet God used their personality to communicate His words. The fact is, our ministry *is* colored by us. We have a great treasure, but it still is contained in an earthen vessel.

This reveals to us our need to purify the vessel. If the vessel is tainted, the ministry will be tainted. If the minister has gaps in his/her character, there will be gaps in his/her ability to deliver a pure message. Yet God has chosen to use us to represent Him to the world and to the church. Wow! That is why He also goes through painstaking lengths to purify us from things that would harm us and taint the ministry of God's Word.

At issue for leaders is the reality that leadership in the Kingdom of God functions quite differently than leadership in the world. In fact, it has even been called the upside-down Kingdom, because the Kingdom of God works opposite to the natural domain. Consider the following examples:

1. Humility: The way up is the way down (see Phil. 2:3-7; 1 Pet. 5:1-7). It is the humble who are exalted and the proud who become abased. If we attempt to lift ourselves up, we stumble; if we get low, we will be exalted by God.

2. Surrender: Letting go is the way to receive (see Mk. 8:34-35; 10:29-30). If we try to save our life, we will lose it. If we let go of our life, we will find it. We must give to get, sow to reap, etc.

3. Brokenness: When you are weak, you are strong (see 2 Cor. 12:9-10). It is when we are at terms with our inadequacy that we come to learn we can confidently rely upon *His* adequacy.

4. Servanthood: The greatest is the servant of all (see Mt. 20:25-28). Great leaders are the ones who are great at servanthood. Give one who is a servant at heart a position of authority, and he will use his position to serve others.

5. Meekness: The meek shall inherit the earth (see Mt. 5:5). If we have to foist our leadership on others, we show that we have none (or that ours is the world's version of leadership). A wise leader is peaceable and easily entreated (see Jas. 3:17).

Next we will look at some of the Lord's schools of character curriculum and how He goes about preparing His leaders for corporateness.

Chapter 8

God's Processes in Preparing His People for Corporateness

God's Character Curriculum of Life

I began writing this section dealing solely with the issues God desires to adjust in leaders in preparing them for more effective leadership. However, it then occurred to me that God is not at all partial. His agenda for leader and saint alike is for us to become conformed to His image. Neither the leader nor the non-leader is exempt from His processes to bring us to that place of conformity to the image of Jesus. The only difference is that leaders have a greater potential to spread their "non-christlikeness" to others. I've observed two errors in regard to this, the irony of which is obvious. One is that non-leaders can feel that they are exempt because they are not leaders. The other is that leaders feel that they are exempt because they are leaders. Judson Cornwall wrote a wonderful little book about this a while back called *Leaders, Eat What You Serve.*

Throughout this section, I will use the inclusive term *saints and overseers* for simplicity, as that is the inclusive term the apostle Paul used in addressing the entire community of Christians in his greeting found in Philippians 1:1 (NAS): "Paul and Timothy, bond-servants of Christ Jesus, to all the saints in Christ Jesus who are in Philippi, including the overseers and deacons."

God's school of character curriculum for saints and overseers occurs in the school of life much more than in any classroom. This school is God's dealing with a man or woman that may endure a lifetime. For unless the character foundation is sufficiently laid, when the heady glory of success comes through our giftings, it will only serve to topple our ministry and lead to our demise. And remember, just as in any school, you keep repeating the test until you pass. Sounds fun, right? But we can take courage from the following Scriptures:

> *Now no chastening seems to be joyful for the present, but painful; nevertheless, afterward it yields the peaceable fruit of righteousness to those who have been trained by it* (Hebrews 12:11).

> *But we have this treasure in earthen vessels, that the excellence of the power may be of God and not of us. ... For our light affliction, which is but for a moment, is working for us a far more exceeding and eternal weight of glory, while we do not look at the things which are seen, but at the things which are not seen. For the things which are seen are temporary, but the things which are not seen are eternal* (2 Corinthians 4:7,17-18).

The School of Brokenness

Brokenness is what rids a man of any confidence in his own soul's resources. We see an unbroken Moses after 40 years of secular training in the finest leadership schools Egypt had to offer. He then realized that he was called to be a deliverer, so he went about trying to knock off the Egyptian army one guy at a time. His efforts only got him banished to the desert. Then we see him after 40 years of desert tempering, and finally, at 80 years of age, we see a man who was called the meekest man on earth. Now he was ready to be used of God in a mighty way. Brokenness made the difference.

One who has been through God's "school of brokenness" is no longer marked by that obstinacy, hardness, and sharpness that are hallmarks of an unbroken man. Meekness is the sign of brokenness. It is Jacob walking with a limp. It is Paul admitting he was a persecutor of the church. Meekness is not the same as weakness; rather, it is characterized by a humble reliance on God's power and strength. Moses relied upon God's power, not his own. We see Moses, not defending himself to his accusers, but rather falling on his face in intercession while God moved dramatically to defend him.

The one who is meek will also exhibit sensitivity toward others. He or she will be approachable and teachable instead of hard and unapproachable. The one who is meek is not arrogantly independent but rather recognizes his/her need for corporateness. The more confidence people have in themselves at the beginning of this school, the longer and harder the breaking will be. But when God accomplishes the work He is after, He can exhibit mighty signs and wonders through such a person because both know that God will get the credit.

God's means and ways of introducing us to the school of broken-ness are as varied and various as there are people. It usually looks like a grave failure within a person's life. But it accomplishes the transforma-tion from self-confidence to God-confidence. He knows just what it takes to bring any one of us to the end of our self. If you are one who has expe-rienced exceptional brokenness or calamity in your life, it just might be an earmark of one of God's special projects.

Akin to brokenness is the school of humility.

The School of Humility

Humility is essential for usefulness in the Kingdom of God. It is especially essential for His apostles and prophets or anyone who recog-nizes the value of team ministry. We must be free from pride so that our ministry does not vaunt self or attract others to us, but looks for the com-mon good and testifies of Jesus, giving glory to Him.

God says that He resists the proud but gives grace to the humble. But humility is not low self-esteem as some have thought. Nor is it sim-ply the absence of pride. It can best be described as an absence of self or a freedom from a preoccupation with self. We must come to know at the heart level and make peace with the fact that, by our flesh, apart from Him, we can accomplish nothing (and at the same time through Him we can do all things) (see Jn. 15:5; Phil. 4:13). One who is humble is free from having to defend himself or explain himself. It is freedom to serve in the lowest or highest position in which God decides to place you. It is not gained by measuring ourselves by ourselves or comparing ourselves among ourselves, but rather, it comes by seeing God!

Isaiah got a glimpse of God and suddenly he had a right perspec-tive of himself (see Is. 6). It resulted in a confession and then a commis-sioning. He did not think of himself more highly than he ought, nor more poorly than he ought, but he had a sober and proper perspective. I do not think that we have the capacity within ourselves of rightly assess-ing our own selves apart from God. This kind of humility is the result of seeing Him.

The next two schools of character building are the "school of of-fence" and the "school of aloneness and rejection." These two schools are specially designed to rid the saint and the overseer alike of the problem of anger and the problem of fear of man. A deeper dealing with these issues can be found in the following chapters where we take an in-depth look at Jonah, the angry prophet, and Jeremiah, the insecure prophet. We must understand that these two things are the biggest hindrances to effective ministry and to a life of righteousness, peace, and joy in the experience of any believer.

The School of Offence

God will allow His "masterpiece in the making" to endure the school of offence because anyone who ministers must be free from offence lest their angry spirit filters through their message and make it unreceivable. Luke 17:1-2 tells us that offence is inevitable in life:

> Then He said to the disciples, "It is impossible that no offenses should come, but woe to him through whom they do come! It would be better for him if a millstone were hung around his neck, and he were thrown into the sea, than that he should offend one of these little ones."

The critical lessons from this Scripture are twofold. First, we *will* have opportunity to be offended and we must not allow it to poison us. Second, we must not be the ones originating the offence. Saints and overseers who minister must always make their "truth" receivable. For example, a primary hindrance to usefulness in prophetic ministry is unresolved anger in the heart of the prophet. It only takes one time of being "torched" by an "angry prophet" to know that a person like that can cause grave offence and defilement.

When the inevitable offence comes to our life, as it does with all, we are told to forgive and not allow it to taint our soul; otherwise, we ourselves will be candidates to defile others with our bitter heart. Hebrews 12:15 (NAS) says it this way: "See to it that no one comes short of the grace of God; that no root of bitterness springing up causes trouble, and by it many be defiled." Scripture also clearly states in James 1:20-21: "For the wrath of man does not produce the righteousness of God. Therefore lay aside all filthiness and overflow of wickedness, and receive with meekness the implanted word, which is able to save your souls." It is wounded people who wound other people.

Of course, the antidote for offence is forgiveness. God calls His servants to be courteous to the obnoxious, loving to the unlovable, and merciful to the unworthy. He expects us to forgive even as He does. The Christ-like believer and leader alike must be an "expert forgiver," and of course, the only way you become an expert at anything is through lots of practice. That is exactly why most leaders-in-training have had ravaging opportunities through life to gather offence and have thereby learned how to swiftly and readily draw upon the grace of God to forgive...and forgive...and forgive.

This revelation hit me like a bolt of lightning one day when I explained to someone who was amazed at my cool, calm manner in dealing with a very offensive person: "I've been burned by experts; this incident is a piece of cake." It is those who have overcome very severely wounding offences and have allowed the grace and forgiveness of God to work deeply in their souls who can remain objective messengers of God without letting their own anger bleed through.

The School of Aloneness and Rejection

The fear of man brings a snare, but he who trusts in the Lord will be exalted (Proverbs 29:25 NAS).

Separation, isolation, and rejection are the sociological effects of the fall of man. Because we are fallen beings, we continue to reject and be rejected and suffer isolation. We are incapable of fully loving and being loved. As a result, we have a large love- and acceptance-shaped hole in our heart that God alone can fill. God has reversed the curse of sin through the cross and so has made provision for us to come into unconditional love and acceptance *in Him*. But we often try to fill that hole in our hearts with the little crumbs of acceptance and approval that man seems to offer.

This is the root of people-pleasing and the fear of man. Yet the saint and the overseer alike must be able to stand alone, unaffected by fear of rejection. We must be free from the snare of the fear of man—that is, to a large extent, the fear of rejection. God may call a child of His to speak an unpopular word or do an unpopular thing. He had Isaiah go naked and barefoot for three years. He called Jeremiah to wear an ox yoke. Hosea was called upon to stay true to his covenant with a harlot wife. We see Jeremiah remaining steadfast to the truth God had spoken to him even when standing in the face of the king who was about to cast him in a pit. It is unpopular to stand against homosexuality in today's culture or to declare that abortion is a murderous abomination to God, which is comparable to the Old Testament sacrifice to Molech. Yet we must be willing to carry God's burden and represent Him, even when it is unpopular.

The primary way God rids us of fear of rejection is by giving us plenty of practice in the face of rejection and aloneness. So often it is, when we have nothing left except Him, that we discover that there is nothing and no one that we need but Him. One of the hardest lessons for some to learn is that God is all we need. We must come to the place where we are able to say, as King David, "Whom have I in heaven but Thee? And besides Thee, I desire nothing on earth" (see Ps. 73:25).

The "leader in the making" will often suffer great rejection in life as God prepares him or her to be invulnerable to it. Every saint needs to learn at the heart level that all he/she really needs is God's acceptance. We must have the courage and strength to stand alone, when need be, and at the same time, we must have the humility and insight to recognize our need of corporateness.

God's agenda of character, integrity, and maturity are very much on His heart for His people. He wants to prepare us to handle His glory without being destroyed by it. He wants to insulate us from harm by building character into us.

I can imagine that by now, some might be saying that it sounds like God is out to kill us. Well, in fact, He is...so that He might live in us, as was Paul's testimony in Galatians 2:20, where he says, "I have been crucified with Christ; it is no longer I who live, but Christ lives in me; and the life which I now live in the flesh I live by faith in the Son of God, who loved me and gave Himself for me."

There are several other common "schools" that God uses to mature His saints and overseers. Next, we will look at the "school of proper relationship," which includes subjects such as discipleship, submission to authority, loyalty, and accountability.

The School of Proper Relationship

In Ephesians 2:19-22, Paul the apostle states that we are no longer alienated, but rather fellow citizens with the saints, that we are being "fitted together" and "built together" into a dwelling of God. To be "fitted together" and "built together" simply means that we are "connected" by relationship with one another.

God intends that we be rightly related to one another. The Scriptures in First John 2:9-11 and 4:19-21 imply that if we want to stay in right relationship with God, we must be about the work of maintaining a right relationship with our brothers and sisters in Christ. This means that the task of building and maintaining right relationships is not an optional sideline, but rather is an essential ingredient of our Christian life.

Independence and isolation are sure signs of unhealthiness or immaturity. Proverbs 18:1 (NAS) states, "He who separates himself seeks his own desire, he quarrels against all sound wisdom." Instead we are to "...grow up in all things into...Christ—from whom the whole body, joined and knit together by what every joint supplies, according to the effective working by which every part does its share, causes growth of the body for the edifying of itself in love" (Eph. 4:15-16).

God is so concerned that we be rightly related to one another that He has inextricably connected His dealings with us to our dealings with one another. For instance, if we don't forgive others, He will not forgive us (see Mk. 11:25-26). The entire law and prophets are summarized in Matthew 22:37-40 as our being rightly related to God and to one another. Being rightly related also speaks to the issue of proper structure and government within the church. Being rightly fitted and held together includes understanding how to relate to spiritual authority and how to properly exercise spiritual authority.

Actually, we are broaching a subject that might provoke some controversy, especially since the principles of authority, submission, discipleship (mentoring), and accountability have been very misunderstood and have lent themselves to abuse by unscrupulous leaders at times. However, they remain truths from Scripture and are a means of maturity in the life of every saint and overseer without partiality.

Much of what we have discussed so far has to do with God's direct dealings with the follower of Jesus. Some of His believers and leaders have been trained out in the "wilderness of life" with no one but God to lead them. Elijah was such a one. Others have the opportunity to learn from mentors like Elijah, as was the case with Elisha. Elisha outshined the others of his day who were enrolled in the "school of the prophets" because he was personally mentored by Elijah.

In fact, most of the great prophetic voices, such as Samuel (by Eli) and Moses (by Jethro), were mentored during significant periods of training in life. A deeper look into Scripture will also reveal that the ones who were alone are the ones who, more often than not, suffered from the lack of relationship that would have kept them in balance. Many would like to fancy themselves as an independent Elijah who could call down fire from heaven or confront the prophets of Baal. But Elijah did not understand the value of a team, and he actually made the mistake of thinking at one point that he was the only one on God's side. In First Kings 19, we see him plunging into a suicidal depression. God had to correct him and tell him that there were 7,000 who had not bowed their knee to Baal. Elisha, on the other hand, learned the lessons that servanthood and submission could teach him, and Elisha did twice the number of miracles that Elijah did.

We need to understand that God wants us to be in relationship, but for the right reasons. He calls us into interdependence, not co-dependence; mutual respect and cooperation, not fear of man and people-pleasing.

The School of Discipleship

Numerous books, organizations, and movements have emerged covering this topic in great detail, and this chapter is not meant to cover every dynamic, balance, and warning that could be addressed. I do want to share, however, some principles I learned as one who has been enriched from various mentor relationships throughout my life, particularly Bishop Bill Hamon and his Network of Prophetic Ministries in regard to prophetic ministry.

Although it is not always possible, one of the ways that God matures His saints and overseers is by placing them under a mentor. Mentoring or discipleship has always been a primary means of training, as promoted in Scripture. (Elijah did it, Jesus did it, John the Baptist did it, Paul the apostle did it and encouraged Timothy to do it. The Great Commission tells us all to do it [see Mt. 28:19-20].)

Actually, one of the New Testament mandates for fivefold ministers is that of being equippers or trainers. Scripture tells us that we can and should be equipped for ministry by existing leaders.

And He Himself gave some to be...prophets...for the equipping of the saints for the work of ministry, for the edifying of the body of Christ (Ephesians 4:11-12).

The Elijah/Elisha Pattern

There are several principles that we can glean from the Elijah/Elisha pattern for mentoring one another. One is that Elisha served his mentor and inherited his mantle. Scripture tells us if we are faithful to make another successful, we will reap our own in due time.

He who is faithful in what is least is faithful also in much.... And if you have not been faithful in what is another man's, who will give you what is your own? (Luke 16:10a,12)

As apprentices, we are called to give ourselves to making our mentor successful. We see Elisha giving himself as Elijah's personal servant for a number of years before he ever did anything else. We see Joshua serving Moses for 40 years before he took up the mantle and led the people. In exchange for our service, we receive training, character formation, and impartation of anointing (sometimes in double measure, as in Elisha's case).

Elisha was a man under authority, and he inherited authority in contrast to Gehazi, Elisha's disciple who did his own thing and inherited leprosy (see 2 Kings 5). Then there was Miriam, who also experienced a bout of leprosy when she spoke against the God-given authority in her brother Moses (see Num. 12).

The School of Spiritual Authority

Anyone who comes to understand how authority works will actually scramble to find authentic authority to submit to. For it is those who are under authority who have authority (see Mt. 8:8-9). Some say, "I am under God's authority alone...." Sorry, it doesn't work that way. In the same way that the apostle John stated that you cannot say you love God if you hate your neighbor (see 1 Jn. 4:20), you also cannot say that you are submitted to God while in rebellion to His delegated authorities on earth.

> *Let every person be in subjection to the governing authorities. For there is no authority except from God, and those which exist are established by God. Therefore he who resists authority has opposed the ordinance of God; and they who have opposed will receive condemnation upon themselves* (Romans 13:1-2 NAS).

There is also an amazing, inevitable pattern of sowing and reaping in respect to authority. (Don't ask me how I discovered this one....) The way that you respect and submit to authority over you becomes the same way you will be treated by those you eventually have the responsibility to exercise authority over. Selah.

First Peter 5 brings further clarity as to how this should be exercised and the fact that authority is not license to "lord" over God's people, so let's take a look at it:

> *Shepherd the flock of God among you, exercising oversight not under compulsion, but voluntarily, according to the will of God; and not for sordid gain, but with eagerness; nor yet as lording it over those allotted to your charge, but proving to be examples to the flock. And when the Chief Shepherd appears, you will receive the unfading crown of glory. You younger men, likewise, be subject to your elders; and all of you, clothe yourselves with humility toward one another, for GOD IS OPPOSED TO THE PROUD, BUT GIVES GRACE TO THE HUMBLE* (1 Peter 5:2-5 NAS).

Yes, Kingdom authority is exercised in a much different way than worldly authority, but God still calls leaders into positions of authority, and Scripture very clearly states we all are to submit to the authorities God places over us.

> *Obey your leaders, and submit to them; for they keep watch over your souls, as those who will give an account. Let them do this with joy and*

not with grief, for this would be unprofitable for you (Hebrews 13:17 NAS).

I know that this is idealistic and that there are numerous angles and circumstances regarding this; however, I believe every leader and saint would be much better off if he/she had a "pastor"—whether that pastor is a pastor, an apostle, or an older prophet. You may ask, "Are there ever extenuating circumstances that would create exceptions?" Of course. But the principles of authority, humility, and accountability should be in evidence in each believer's life, one way or another.

Every individual minister, as well as every individual saint, must recognize the need to connect with the larger body of Christ. Psalm 133 states that where the brethren dwell together in unity, there the Lord commands a blessing. We must always recognize we are part of a body and are not designed to exist alone. A prophetically gifted person may never learn to come into right relationship to the rest of the body of Christ and still be a prophet, but the sad fact is that this person's usefulness in the church will be stunted and limited.

I strongly believe that it is essential for believers, prophets particularly, to recognize their need for apostles. Likewise, apostles must recognize their need for prophets, as these two ministries together form the foundation for a properly built church (see Eph. 2:20). One of the vital issues of the church in this hour is destined to be how to properly relate as team ministries within the body of Christ as we see apostolic team ministry emerging once again in the earth. This will take prophets who have the courage to stand alone (when need be) but who also have the humility and insight to recognize the value of corporateness.

The next two chapters deal in a more specific way with the two biggest hurdles to corporateness that are common to the human experience—anger and fear of man. To do so, we will examine the personality profiles of two Old Testament prophets—Jonah, the angry prophet, and Jeremiah, the fearful prophet—and we will learn how they managed their problems.

Chapter 9

Overcoming Obstacles to Corporateness, Part 1

Jonah the Angry Prophet

Introduction

Jonah was an Old Testament prophet who had a problem with anger, bitterness, and unforgiveness. His life and ministry were severely affected by his unresolved anger. He was a man who had the words of God, but not the heart of God. He led one of the most successful city-wide revivals in Scripture, yet he ended in failure because of his anger and bitterness of heart.

> Then God saw their works, that they turned from their evil way; and God relented from the disaster that He had said He would bring upon them, and He did not do it. But it displeased Jonah exceedingly, and he became angry. ... Then the Lord said, "Is it right for you to be angry?" ... Then God said to Jonah, "Is it right for you to be angry about the plant?" And he said, "It is right for me to be angry, even to death!" (Jonah 3:10–4:1,4,9)

One of the primary hindrances to usefulness in prophetic ministry (or other areas of ministry for that matter) is unresolved anger in the heart of the believer. The prophet is called to be a spokesman for God, but he must take care to communicate in such a way as to make His truth receivable. Anger in the heart of a prophet does not communicate God's heart; rather, it makes His "truth" abrasive and unreceivable, and it can, in fact, even bring a degree of defilement those to whom he ministers.

See to it...that no root of bitterness springing up causes trouble, and by it many be defiled (Hebrews 12:15 NAS).

The Background

God had called Jonah to minister to the Ninevites.

Now the word of the Lord came to Jonah the son of Amittai, saying, "Arise, go to Nineveh, that great city, and cry out against it; for their wickedness has come up before Me" (Jonah 1:1-2).

To fully grasp the dynamic involved here, it is important to know the general mood of Israel toward Nineveh. Nineveh was the capital of the Assyrian Empire. It was known as "the Robber City" because the Ninevites would overrun and rob other countries to enrich themselves. They were responsible for a number of Israel's greatest disasters. In the eighth and seventh centuries B.C., they invaded Palestine again and again, looting and burning cities, laying waste the countryside, and deporting the inhabitants. The inhabitants of Nineveh were more hated by the Israelites than the people of any other city.

Nineveh was also a very immoral place. It was originally founded by Nimrod, which gave it ancient occultic origins. The city itself was named after the pagan goddess Nina and was a major center of false worship. The goddess Nina was the Assyrian rendition of the Babylonian Ishtar, the Canaanite Ashtoreth, and the Egyptian Isis—the goddess of fertility, love, and war. Its worship was characterized by lurid and perverse immorality and violence.

Israel—the "remnant of God," the "holy nation"—originally understood that they were called to be a redemptive agent in the earth through whom grace and truth would one day reach all men (see Is. 42, 60, 61, etc.) However, in the years after the Exile, there grew up in Israel a spirit of bitterness and vengefulness toward other lands. The nation had endured so much at the hands of enemies that the people had little inclination to keep alive the vision of the nation of Israel as God's servant through whom redemptive truth would come. Their most passionate desire was that God's wrath should utterly consume all their enemies.

Jonah's Rebellion

Into this context, we find Jonah called upon to prophesy to Nineveh, warning it of its destruction. But Jonah despised the Ninevites. The first evidence of Jonah's poor attitude comes from his refusal to obey God in Jonah 1:3a:

But Jonah arose to flee to Tarshish from the presence of the Lord.

The reason, however, is revealed in Jonah 4:2-3. After realizing that God was going to show mercy, he was angry and said to the Lord,

> *... "Ah, Lord, was not this what I said when I was still in my country? Therefore I fled previously to Tarshish; for I know that You are a gracious and merciful God, slow to anger and abundant in lovingkindness, One who relents from doing harm. Therefore now, O Lord, please take my life from me, for it is better for me to die than to live!"*

His refusal to minister to the Ninevites was actually because he hated them and didn't want God to save them. He knew that if they responded rightly to his warnings, God's anger would turn into mercy.

Anger is often at the root of isolation and rebellion and is ultimately rebellion against God. Though some will point to the righteous anger of God, the anger that originates from the heart of man is not able to accomplish God's purposes (see Jas. 1:20 NAS). It is vital for us to understand the difference between reflecting God's "righteous indignation" and displaying the anger that originates from the human heart.

God's Righteous Indignation

- When we reflect God's righteous indignation, there should be no personal loss or gain involved (no personal ax to grind).
- It should come through one's "spirit" apart from our soul (emotion).
- It is in keeping with God's amazing forbearance and continuous desire to be reconciled.

The Anger of Man

- Any anger that originates from our own personal wounds should automatically be suspect.
- The anger of man is judgmental and condemning instead of willing to be reconciliatory.
- The anger of man most often has compulsiveness behind it. It lacks peace.

But if you have bitter jealousy and selfish ambition in your heart, do not be arrogant and so lie against the truth. This wisdom is not that which comes down from above, but is earthly, natural, demonic. For where jealousy and selfish ambition exist, there is disorder and every evil thing. But the wisdom from above is first pure, then peaceable, gentle, reasonable, full of mercy and good fruits, unwavering, without hypocrisy. And the seed whose fruit is righteousness is sown in peace by those who make peace (James 3:14-18 NAS).

When we as prophetic ministers have unresolved anger, bitterness, and offence in our heart:

- Our "spirit" or attitude will filter through our message.
- Who we are will often speak as loud or louder than what we say.
- A contentious attitude will often be what makes our message unreceivable.
- When we fail to mingle truth with grace and judgment with mercy, we fail to rightly represent the Lord and His Kingdom. A messenger with a warning must always know God's heart of compassion—that God *always* wants repentance and consequent restoration, reconciliation, and healing.

Old Testament

Then the Lord passed by in front of him and proclaimed, "The Lord, the Lord God, compassionate and gracious, slow to anger, and abounding in lovingkindness and truth; who keeps lovingkindness for thousands, who forgives iniquity, transgression and sin; yet He will by no means leave the guilty unpunished, visiting the iniquity of fathers on the children and on the grandchildren to the third and fourth generations" (Exodus 34:6-7 NAS).

New Testament

But they did not receive Him, because His face was set for the journey to Jerusalem. And when His disciples James and John saw this, they said, "Lord, do You want us to command fire to come down from heaven and consume them, just as Elijah did?" But He turned and rebuked them, and said, "You do not know what manner of spirit you are of. For the Son of Man did not come to destroy men's lives but to save them." And they went to another village (Luke 9:53-56).

Jonah's Second Chance

Of course, Jonah's rebellion led him to the bottom of the sea in the belly of a great fish. Anger will always lead us on a path down into torment and captivity. After having been disciplined by God to within an inch of his life, the word of the Lord came again to Jonah in chapter 3:

Now the word of the Lord came to Jonah the second time, saying, "Arise, go to Nineveh, that great city, and preach to it the message that I tell you." So Jonah arose and went to Nineveh, according to the word of the Lord. Now Nineveh was an exceedingly great city, a three-day journey in extent (Jonah 3:1-3).

However, Jonah's trip to Nineveh was out of mere compliance rather than from any conviction or burden. There had not been a change in Jonah's heart, and he had not dealt with the root issues that were feeding his anger. Stopping bad fruit requires dealing with the root.

Roots of Bitterness

See to it that no one comes short of the grace of God; that no root of bitterness springing up causes trouble, and by it many be defiled (Hebrews 12:15 NAS).

John and Paula Sandford define bitterness in the following way: "Roots of bitterness are based in offence and unforgiveness toward a particular person or group that has been allowed to remain in the heart, thereafter effecting our ability to love and forgive others."[1]

Roots of bitterness are caused by unresolved offence (unforgiveness).
- Forgiveness is not an option (see Lk. 17:1-10).
- Forgiveness is not pretending we were not sinned against.
- Forgiveness is an undeserved gift from God.

Roots of bitterness are caused by unhealed wounds.
- Wounds from others.
- Wounds from ourselves.
- Wounding events of life.

There are serious personal as well as ministerial consequences to unresolved anger. The progressive consequences of anger in Jonah were rebellion, isolation, bitterness, and ultimately depression and thoughts of suicide.

"Therefore now, O Lord, please take my life from me, for it is better for me to die than to live!" ... Then God said to Jonah, "Is it right for you to be angry about the plant?" And he said, "It is right for me to be angry, even to death!" (Jonah 4:3,9)

Personal Consequences of Unresolved Anger

- Physical: colitis, arthritis, toxic goiters, ulcers, cancer, etc.
- Spiritual

---

1. Taken from a seminar given in Phoenix, Arizona, in 1983.

1. Inability to Love God

If someone says, "I love God," and hates his brother, he is a liar; for he who does not love his brother whom he has seen, how can he love God whom he has not seen? And this commandment we have from Him: that he who loves God must love his brother also (1 John 4:20-21).

2. Inability to Receive Forgiveness From God

"Therefore I say to you, all things for which you pray and ask, believe that you have received them, and they shall be granted you. And whenever you stand praying, forgive, if you have anything against anyone; so that your Father also who is in heaven may forgive you your transgressions. [But if you do not forgive, neither will your Father who is in heaven forgive your transgressions]" (Mark 11:24-26 NAS).

3. Spiritual Torment and Imprisonment

Then Peter came and said to Him, "Lord, how often shall my brother sin against me and I forgive him? Up to seven times?" Jesus said to him, "I do not say to you, up to seven times, but up to seventy times seven. For this reason the kingdom of heaven may be compared to a certain king who wished to settle accounts with his slaves. ...his lord said to him, 'You wicked slave, I forgave you all that debt because you entreated me. Should you not also have had mercy on your fellow slave, even as I had mercy on you?' And his lord, moved with anger, handed him over to the torturers until he should repay all that was owed him. So shall My heavenly Father also do to you, if each of you does not forgive his brother from your heart" (Matthew 18:21-23, 32-35 NAS).

Ministry Consequences of Unresolved Anger

After we have a peek into God's personal discipline of Jonah in chapter 4 and His object lesson with the withered plant, we never hear from Jonah again. His notoriety comes from the belly of the fish incident, but one cannot help but wonder why a man with such a dramatic encounter with God and His word trailed off into obscurity. He was a man who had a very fruitful revival campaign but, nevertheless, allowed his unresolved anger to render him personally depressed and ministerially neutralized from any further work for God.

Conclusion

Let us take to heart the exhortation that Paul gave to the Ephesian Christians that applies to all Christians and that most certainly applies to any who would be a spokesman for God:

> *Let no unwholesome word proceed from your mouth, but only such a word as is good for edification according to the need of the moment, that it may give grace to those who hear. And do not grieve the Holy Spirit of God, by whom you were sealed for the day of redemption. Let all bitterness and wrath and anger and clamor and slander be put away from you, along with all malice. And be kind to one another, tender-hearted, forgiving each other, just as God in Christ also has forgiven you* (Ephesians 4:29-32 NAS).

Chapter 10

Overcoming Obstacles to Corporateness, Part 2

Jeremiah, the Insecure Prophet

The fear of man brings a snare, but he who trusts in the Lord will be exalted (Proverbs 29:25 NAS).

...if prophecy, let us prophesy in proportion to our faith (Romans 12:6).

Introduction

Jeremiah was an Old Testament prophet who was significantly used of the Lord during a time of deep spiritual darkness in Israel's history. The Book of Jeremiah reveals an interesting series of insights into the personality of Jeremiah, who as a young man in the beginning of his ministry, exhibited fears, insecurities, and a real aversion to the numerous rejections his ministry exposed him to. He was by nature subjective, reticent, and introspective:

> Then I said, "Alas, Lord God! Behold, I do not know how to speak, because I am a youth." ... "Do not be afraid of them, for I am with you to deliver you," declares the Lord (Jeremiah 1:6,8 NAS).

> Woe to me, my mother, that you have borne me as a man of strife and a man of contention to all the land...because of Thy hand upon me I sat alone, for Thou didst fill me with indignation (Jeremiah 15:10,17 NAS).

Jeremiah was one of the most sensitive of the prophets:

O Lord, Thou hast deceived me and I was deceived; Thou hast over-come me and prevailed. I have become a laughingstock all day long; everyone mocks me. For each time I speak, I cry aloud; I proclaim vio-lence and destruction, because for me the word of the Lord has result-ed in reproach and derision all day long. But if I say, "I will not remember Him or speak anymore in His name," then in my heart it becomes like a burning fire shut up in my bones; and I am weary of holding it in, and I cannot endure it. ... Cursed be the day when I was born; let the day not be blessed when my mother bore me! ... Why did I ever come forth from the womb to look on trouble and sorrow, so that my days have been spent in shame? (Jeremiah 20:7-9,14,18 NAS)

Contained within his story are many of the significant antidotes for insecurity that God gives. Consider, for example, this strong promise:

Therefore, thus says the Lord, "If you return, then I will restore you—before Me you will stand; and if you extract the precious from the worthless, you will become My spokesman. They for their part may turn to you, but as for you, you must not turn to them. Then I will make you to this people a fortified wall of bronze; and though they fight against you, they will not prevail over you; for I am with you to save you and deliver you," declares the Lord. "So I will deliver you from the hand of the wicked, and I will redeem you from the grasp of the violent" (Jeremiah 15:19-21 NAS).

He ultimately became one of the most courageous of the prophets.

And when Jeremiah finished speaking all that the Lord had com-manded him to speak to all the people, the priests and the prophets and all the people seized him, saying, "You must die!" ... Then Jere-miah spoke to all the officials and to all the people, saying, "The Lord sent me to prophesy against this house and against this city all the words that you have heard. Now therefore amend your ways and your deeds, and obey the voice of the Lord your God; and the Lord will change His mind about the misfortune which He has pronounced against you. But as for me, behold, I am in your hands; do with me as is good and right in your sight. Only know for certain that if you put me to death, you will bring innocent blood on yourselves, and on this city, and on its inhabitants; for truly the Lord has sent me to you to speak all these words in your hearing" (Jeremiah 26:8,12-15 NAS).

What Jeremiah Had to Face

Jeremiah was ridiculed, rejected by family and friends, thrown into jail at one point, and into a mud pit another time. He was called to speak very unpleasant prophetic words to the king and other officials. He had to face and overcome his fear in order to be effective for God. Through the Lord, he was ultimately able to replace his fear with an unusual level of faith-induced courage.

It is in our weaknesses that Christ's strength is perfected, as Paul the apostle explained in Second Corinthians 12:9 (NAS): "And He has said to me, 'My grace is sufficient for you, for power is perfected in weakness.' Most gladly, therefore, I will rather boast about my weaknesses, that the power of Christ may dwell in me." The anger-prone become expert forgivers (humility); the fearful become most courageous (faith).

There were two primary kinds of fear that Jeremiah had to face from which he had to gain freedom. They were the fear of loss and the fear of rejection.

Freedom From Fear of Loss

Jeremiah had to overcome his fear of loss. God calls us to replace our fear of loss with faith in His provision. Our own fears become our bondages. It is release and surrender that produces security and rest. Total surrender requires trust in *Him*!

Scripture calls us to surrender the following:

- Possessions

For what does it profit a man to gain the whole world, and forfeit his soul? (Mark 8:36 NAS)

- Reputation

For what shall a man give in exchange for his soul? For whoever is ashamed of Me and My words in this adulterous and sinful generation, the Son of Man will also be ashamed of him when He comes in the glory of His Father with the holy angels (Mark 8:37-38 NAS).

- Selfishness

And He summoned the multitude with His disciples, and said to them, "If anyone wishes to come after Me, let him deny himself, and take up his cross, and follow Me. For whoever wishes to save his life shall lose it; but whoever loses his life for My sake and the gospel's shall save it" (Mark 8:34-35 NAS).

- Needs

For after all these things the Gentiles seek. For your heavenly Father knows that you need all these things. But seek first the kingdom of God and His righteousness, and all these things shall be added to you (Matthew 6:32-33).

- Relationships

He who loves father or mother more than Me is not worthy of Me. And he who loves son or daughter more than Me is not worthy of Me. And he who does not take his cross and follow after Me is not worthy of Me. He who finds his life will lose it, and he who loses his life for My sake will find it (Matthew 10:37-39).

- Life Itself

Since then the children share in flesh and blood, He Himself likewise also partook of the same, that through death He might render power-less him who had the power of death, that is, the devil; and might deliver those who through fear of death were subject to slavery all their lives (Hebrews 2:14-15 NAS).

And they overcame him because of the blood of the Lamb and because of the word of their testimony, and they did not love their life even to death (Revelation 12:11 NAS).

Freedom From Fear of Rejection

Jeremiah had to face rejection and loss because of the message he carried. He was called to speak against the moral depravity of the culture and the people he lived with. (If you're going to be a martyr, do it for a worthy cause.) Six of the seven kings who reigned during his ministry participated in the sins of Manasseh, as well as the people.

Manasseh...did evil in the sight of the Lord, according to the abominations of the nations whom the Lord dispossessed before the sons of Israel. For he rebuilt the high places...he erected altars for Baal and made an Asherah...and worshiped all the host of heaven and served them. And he built altars in the house of the Lord...he built altars for all the host of heaven in the two courts of the house of the Lord. And he made his son pass through the fire, practiced witchcraft and used divination, and dealt with mediums and spiritists. He did much evil in the sight of the Lord provoking Him to anger. Then he set the carved image of Asherah that he had made, in the house of...the Lord...and Manasseh seduced them to do evil more than the nations whom the Lord destroyed before the sons of Israel (2 Kings 21:1-9 NAS).

Likewise, Amon, Jehoahaz, Jehoiakim, Jehoiachin, and Zedekiah did evil in the sight of the Lord, as their fathers had done (see 2 Kings 21:19-22; 23:32,37; 24:9,19). The nation had totally forsaken God. They were worshiping Baal and Asherah, the worship of which was morally depraved and wicked. They were morally and spiritually deceived.

Jeremiah was called upon to stand alone in the face of rejection:

- He was rejected by his neighbors.

But I was like a gentle lamb led to the slaughter; and I did not know that they had devised plots against me, saying, "Let us destroy the tree with its fruit, and let us cut him off from the land of the living, that his name be remembered no more." ... Therefore thus says the Lord concerning the men of Anathoth, who seek your life, saying, "Do not prophesy in the name of the Lord, that you might not die at our hand" (Jeremiah 11:19,21 NAS).

- He was rejected by his family.

For even your brothers and the household of your father, even they have dealt treacherously with you, even they have cried aloud after you. Do not believe them, although they may say nice things to you (Jeremiah 12:6 NAS).

- He was rejected by priests and prophets.

When Pashhur the priest...heard Jeremiah prophesying these things, Pashhur had Jeremiah the prophet beaten, and put him in the stocks that were at the upper Benjamin Gate... (Jeremiah 20:1-2 NAS).

- He was rejected by his friends.

For I have heard the whispering of many, "Terror on every side! Denounce him; yes, let us denounce him!" All my trusted friends, watching for my fall... (Jeremiah 20:10 NAS).

- He was rejected by all the people.

And when Jeremiah finished speaking all that the Lord had commanded him to speak to all the people, the priests and the prophets and all the people seized him, saying, "You must die!" (Jeremiah 26:8 NAS)

- He was rejected by the king.

And it came about, when Jehudi had read three or four columns, the king cut it with a scribe's knife and threw it into the fire that was in the brazier, until all the scroll was consumed in the fire that was in the brazier (Jeremiah 36:23 NAS).

- He never married.

The word of the Lord also came to me saying, "You shall not take a wife for yourself nor have sons or daughters in this place" (Jeremiah 16:1-2 NAS).

Rejection is the sociological result of the fall of man. The wounds of rejection are inevitable in everyone's experience, simply because of the fact that ever since Adam, we have been incapable of truly giving to one another the unconditional love and acceptance that we so desperately need. So, although we all must deal with the issue of rejection to some degree or other, it is vitally important that the leader, as a spokesman for God, deal with the rejection issue, for he may reap more than his share of rejection as he bears reproach for the sake of Christ.

God's Antidote for Rejection

As we survey the Book of Jeremiah, we find several very important means by which healing and courage came to Jeremiah.

- Intimacy: The healing and courage Jeremiah needed came through intimacy with God.

Thus says the Lord, "Let not a wise man boast of his wisdom, and let not the mighty man boast of his might, let not a rich man boast of his riches; but let him who boasts boast of this, that he understands and knows Me, that I am the Lord who exercises lovingkindness, justice, and righteousness on earth; for I delight in these things," declares the Lord (Jeremiah 9:23-24 NAS).

- Acceptance: He found healing and courage through acceptance from God.

"For I know the plans that I have for you," declares the Lord, "plans for welfare and not for calamity to give you a future and a hope. Then you will call upon Me and come and pray to Me, and I will listen to you. And you will seek Me and find Me, when you search for Me with all your heart. And I will be found by you," declares the Lord... (Jeremiah 29:11-14 NAS).

- Belonging and Identity: He found healing and courage through his belonging and identity in God.

Therefore, thus says the Lord, "If you return, then I will restore you—before Me you will stand; and if you extract the precious from the worthless, You will become My spokesman. They for their part may turn to you, but as for you, you must not turn to them" (Jeremiah 15:19 NAS).

- Destiny: He found healing and courage through discovering God had a destiny for him.

Now the word of the Lord came to me saying, "Before I formed you in the womb I knew you, and before you were born I consecrated you; I have appointed you a prophet to the nations" (Jeremiah 1:4-5 NAS).

- Favor: He found healing and courage through the joy of experiencing God's favor.

And the word of the Lord came to me saying, "What do you see, Jeremiah?" And I said, "I see a rod of an almond tree." Then the Lord said to me, "You have seen well, for I am watching over My word to perform it" (Jeremiah 1:11-12 NAS).

- Defense: He found healing and courage through knowing God was his defender.

But the Lord said to me, "Do not say, 'I am a youth,' because everywhere I send you, you shall go, and all that I command you, you shall speak. Do not be afraid of them, for I am with you to deliver you," declares the Lord (Jeremiah 1:7-8 NAS).

"And I will make you to this people a fortified bronze wall; and they will fight against you, but they shall not prevail against you; for I am with you to save you and deliver you," says the Lord. "I will deliver you from the hand of the wicked, and I will redeem you from the grip of the terrible" (Jeremiah 15:20-21).

For the New Testament saint, God has provided the ultimate antidote for rejection through *His* acceptance that comes through the grace of God. Acceptance has now come to us as the work of the cross of Christ reversed the effects and consequences of the fall of man.

Now all these things are from God, who reconciled us to Himself through Christ, and gave us the ministry of reconciliation, namely, that God was in Christ reconciling the world to Himself, not counting their trespasses against them, and He has committed to us the word of reconciliation. Therefore, we are ambassadors for Christ, as though God were entreating through us; we beg you on behalf of Christ, be reconciled to God (2 Corinthians 5:18-20 NAS).

Wherefore, accept one another, just as Christ also accepted us to the glory of God (Romans 15:7 NAS).

God has already given us what we need in His great and precious promises, and we need to appropriate that provision into our lives by faith. In fact, without faith it is impossible to please Him (see Heb. 11:6). We must learn, then, how to let fear be replaced by faith.

Faith Comes by...

let go of fear, choose faith

- Hearing

So faith comes from hearing, and hearing by the word of Christ (Romans 10:17 NAS).

- Impartation

But to each one is given the manifestation of the Spirit for the common good. For to one is given the word of wisdom through the Spirit, and to another the word of knowledge according to the same Spirit; to another faith by the same Spirit, and to another gifts of healing by the one Spirit (1 Corinthians 12:7-9 NAS).

- Experience

growth process

I have been young, and now I am old; Yet I have not seen the righteous forsaken, or his descendants begging bread (Psalm 37:25 NAS).

- Renewing the Mind

And do not be conformed to this world, but be transformed by the renewing of your mind, that you may prove what the will of God is, that which is good and acceptable and perfect (Romans 12:2 NAS).

God calls us to bring every thought captive to the obedience of Christ.

1. We must replace thoughts of *fear* with *truth.*

And you shall know the truth, and the truth shall make you free (John 8:32 NAS).

"For I know the plans that I have for you," declares the Lord, "plans for welfare and not for calamity to give you a future and a hope" (Jeremiah 29:11 NAS).

2. We must replace thoughts of *fear* with *love.*

There is no fear in love; but perfect love casts out fear, because fear involves punishment, and the one who fears is not perfected in love (1 John 4:18 NAS).

3. We must replace thoughts of *fear* with *trust in God's promises.*

Grace and peace be multiplied to you in the knowledge of God and of Jesus our Lord, as His divine power has given to us all things that pertain to life and godliness, through the knowledge of Him who called us by glory and virtue, by which have been given to us exceedingly great and precious promises, that through these you may be partakers of the divine nature, having escaped the corruption that is in the world through lust (2 Peter 1:2-4).

Jeremiah put great confidence in who God is and what He had promised.

Ah Lord God! Behold, Thou hast made the heavens and the earth by Thy great power and by Thine outstretched arm! Nothing is too difficult for Thee, who showest lovingkindness to thousands, but repayest the iniquity of fathers into the bosom of their children after them, O great and mighty God. The Lord of hosts is His name; great in counsel and mighty in deed, whose eyes are open to all the ways of the sons of men, giving to everyone according to his ways and according to the fruit of his deeds (Jeremiah 32:17-19 NAS).

This I recall to my mind, therefore I have hope. The Lord's lovingkindnesses indeed never cease, for His compassions never fail. They are new every morning; great is Thy faithfulness. "The Lord is my portion," says my soul, "therefore I have hope in Him." The Lord is good to those who wait for Him, to the person who seeks Him (Lamentations 3:21-25 NAS).

As Jeremiah came to the end of his life, having seen God show Himself strong on his behalf and fulfill the words He had spoken to him over and over again, he gave us an example of a prophet who didn't care what anyone thought, for he had learned the secret of being a God pleaser instead of a people pleaser. Jeremiah, the insecure prophet, had become Jeremiah, the courageous champion of God!

Chapter 11

The Integrity of the Building

Apostolic/Prophetic Team Ministry

If the church is to fulfill the mandate God has given that we be "one body," we must enter into a better understanding and practice of team ministry. Again, although these principles apply to saint and overseer alike, it is of vital importance to the building of the church that leaders recognize their need for corporateness and team ministry.

The concept of team ministry can be found in as fundamental of a place as the Godhead Itself. God Himself functions as a team: the Father, Son, and Holy Spirit. Team is a very integral part of God's nature. To be a team player, however, presses us into a whole new dimension of character issues, such as loyalty, humility, and deference, while dealing with our issues of jealousy, competition, insecurity, and desire for recognition.

As a football player in high school, I learned how important it is for each person to fulfill his part for the good of the team. As a tight end, I would sometimes serve the team as a lineman and other times would go out for a pass. Sometimes I would be in the limelight as the guy who caught the pass and ran for the yardage, while other times my part was to knock out the guy in front of me so that our guy with the ball could go for the yardage. If our team made progress, I was successful–if our team did not, I was not.

God desires to bring into the body of Christ a level of unity and team ministry that is significantly lacking right now. But change is almost always resisted, even if it is change for the better. Change takes us out of our comfort zone into the unfamiliar. Most people will strive to stay in the familiar, even if it is bad, just because it is familiar. As was mentioned in Chapter 6, the historic trend has always been for the current restoration "movement" to have within it persons who will resist the next thing God does. There are always some who make the transition into the next thing and others who resist and harden their position, unwilling to embrace change.

So we must ask ourselves the following questions: "What does the current restoration of apostolic ministry imply regarding change?" and "How will the prophets that have emerged in the last two decades respond to it?"

The prophetic movement saw its ministers breaking free of "man-made" restraints and issues pertaining to fear of man. It took a disregard for structures that were not of God and a willingness to "buck the system" and go against the tide. That, of course, can produce the proverbial pendulum swing to the opposite and equally negative extreme of independence and isolation if it is not brought into certain boundaries and limits. Some of the boundaries that God is putting into place is the emergence of proper government and accountability within the body of Christ and a greater understanding of the value of team ministry—one of the specific characteristics of the emerging apostolic movement. What God needs are leaders and saints who can embrace submission one to another and become co-laborers so that together they will be foundational to the church God wants to build.

Team ministry will always produce a greater capacity for progress. Many of the kinds of things that God winked at in the past are now being challenged—specifically, the independence and lack of relationship. Relationships are so very essential to God's end-time purposes.

In addition to the team ministry test, another test that the current saints and leaders must pass is whether they can embrace a builder mentality, which is the driving motive in the heart of the apostolic. It is true that a builder must first clear the building site of the clutter that hinders the proper building, but then the builder wants to *build* something. Many of today's prophets are willing to embrace the first half of Jeremiah's call to root out, pull down, and destroy without realizing that they also need to follow the rest of the call by building and planting (see Jer. 1:10).

These are a few of the other mind-sets that have found root in some prophetic circles *that must change*:

- Anything with structure is bad.
- Traditional church as we know it is to be rejected and written off.

- The implication that anything governmental is false. (By default, this includes pastors, since the common word in our church culture for the person in "government" in the church is *pastor*.)

There are actually many emerging apostles that are operating under cover as pastors, although it seems that God is also recruiting apostles from other arenas, such as business because of their leadership skills and sports because of their team mentality. If we can, for just a moment, lay aside labels, we will see that the real issue is government. Prophets will have to co-operate with government if they want to be optimally useful in what is coming around the bend. Prophets need not reject and condemn government; they need to arise together with apostles and become government! Having said that, I will add that we must also resist the notion that only apostles or pastors can function in government.

Although in the previous section of this book I offered fairly strongly defined descriptions of the apostle and the prophet, it is important to realize there are many blends and overlaps in the definitions of these callings. For instance, Paul told Timothy, who was pastoring as an apostle, to do the work of an evangelist.

The fact is that if each of the fivefold ministries is doing its equipping responsibility, each member of the body will be trained into that ministry's particular grace gifting (see Eph. 4:11-12). For example, an evangelist should be equipping the church (i.e., every member) to be evangelistic. The same follows with the prophet; he/she will activate the prophetic within each member, etc. Note: not all believers are prophets, but each should have some prophetic quality about them if he/she is to be Christ-like. Therefore, to be a fully developed Christian, we need ✗ influence and equipping from all five of the offices.

If this is true, every leader and every saint should have some of each of the fivefold ministries in him or her, but each person will obviously have the strongest gifting in one particular ministry calling. This doesn't eliminate that believer's responsibility in the other areas. It would be wrong for me, for instance, to say, "Well, I'm a prophet; therefore, I can't/shouldn't/don't need to be evangelistic."

In reality, what we have are prophetically gifted apostles, apostolically oriented prophets, pastorally oriented apostles, evangelistic pastors, prophetic teachers, teaching prophets, etc. So then, the prophet who has had exposure to the apostle's influence will have a builder's burden, and the evangelist who has been open to the pastor's burden will care about follow-up with the "fish" he caught.

It is important to acknowledge, however, the unique relationship and placement of the apostle and prophet. The church is described as being "built on the foundation of the apostles and prophets" together as the foundation (see Eph. 2:20). A church without both foundational influences will never be all that God intended it to be. These two ministries need each other. A great example of builders and prophets working together is found in Ezra's day where it was said:

> So the elders of the Jews built, and they prospered through the prophesying of Haggai the prophet and Zechariah the son of Iddo. And they built and finished it, according to the commandment of the God of Israel... (Ezra 6:14).

When apostles and prophets find the grace to be fitted and joined together and work together for the common good of His Kingdom, the building can move forward and be finished. It will become a glorious house in preparation for His return.

I'm now going to venture into some experiential hypotheses that could be controversial. As to the relationship between the apostle and prophet, a very functional principle (though not a hard-and-fast rule) is that subjectivity is to be submitted to objectivity. The principle goes like this: The subjectivity of the Spirit is submitted to the objectivity of the Word; the subjectivity of the female (in marriage) is submitted to the objectivity of the male; and the subjectivity of the prophetic is submitted to the objectivity of the apostolic.

I'm assuming that we all understand that there are exceptional situations, as any marriage counselor worth his or her salt would have to admit. For instance, in marriage, a wise husband will defer to his wife when she has the mind of the Lord concerning a matter. This principle simply establishes the fact that a team needs a leader. Apostolic team ministry models in the New Testament, for instance, show Paul leading the team and James being the chief apostle in Jerusalem.

For those who have problems with one person being the "head," all I can tell you is that anything with more than one head is a monster. But again, using the marriage analogy, the husband who does not listen to his wife's intuitive wisdom is simply foolish. This does not take away from the fact that the apostle and prophet need to function together as a team. For instance, ideally, the apostle receives revelation from the prophet and knows what to do with it for the furtherance of the Kingdom. The prophet also has the ability (as we see in the case of Haggai and Zechariah during Ezra's day) to stir and motivate the people to action. That is why the apostle needs to recognize the gift that the prophet is to him and the work. I also think God deliberately will not let any one of us get everything we need directly from Him so that we will learn interdependence.

Along with this and almost as a paradox to it, God will also not let any one person fully take the place that He alone is to fulfill in every believer's life. We are after the goal of leading people to secure, undistracted devotion to Christ Jesus (see 1 Cor. 7:35). As leaders work together to deposit their portion of the revelation of Christ into the saints that we serve, we will lead them to devotion to Christ, not devotion to us as leaders or overseers. Our ultimate goal is not to draw submission unto ourselves, but lead people to submission to the Head, which is Christ Jesus.

Suggested Prophetic Protocol and Accountability Within the Local Church

And let two or three prophets speak, and let the others pass judgment. But if a revelation is made to another who is seated, let the first keep silent. For you can all prophesy one by one, so that all may learn and all may be exhorted; and the spirits of prophets are subject to prophets; for God is not a God of confusion but of peace, as in all the churches of the saints (1 Corinthians 14:29-33 NAS).

To even address the issue of proper prophetic protocol within the local church is difficult simply due to the fact there are such a wide variety of situations, levels of maturity, and forms of church government being addressed. Readers of this book undoubtedly range all the way from budding prophesiers to internationally recognized prophets/ prophetesses. In some cases, there are those who are very acquainted with prophetic revelation but are not as yet proficient at exercising the vocal gift of "prophesying." Again, the number of variations of prophetic procedures are probably as many as the number of kinds of churches. There are also, of course, a large variety of approaches to the release of prophetic. Consequently, while presenting the following as a suggested "procedure" to follow, we must also reach to a deeper issue of the motives, attitude, and character of the one who would prophesy. We see a very valuable part of the character issue of humility and subjection to leadership addressed in the following verses from Peter's first Epistle:

Therefore, I exhort the elders among you, as your fellow elder and witness of the sufferings of Christ, and a partaker also of the glory that is to be revealed, shepherd the flock of God among you, exercising oversight not under compulsion, but voluntarily, according to the will of God; and not for sordid gain, but with eagerness; nor yet as lording it over those allotted to your charge, but proving to be examples to the flock. And when the Chief Shepherd appears, you will receive the unfading crown of glory. You younger men, likewise, be subject to your elders; and all of you, clothe yourselves with humility toward one another, for GOD IS OPPOSED TO THE PROUD, BUT GIVES GRACE TO THE HUMBLE. Humble yourselves, therefore, under the mighty hand of God, that He may exalt you at the proper time (1 Peter 5:1-6 NAS).

It is important to understand that God Himself established government in the church. It is important, then, to properly relate to that government. The following Scriptures speak to the issue very clearly.

Let every person be in subjection to the governing authorities. For there is no authority except from God, and those which exist are established by God (Romans 13:1 NAS).

Obey your leaders, and submit to them; for they keep watch over your souls, as those who will give an account. Let them do this with joy and not with grief, for this would be unprofitable for you (Hebrews 13:17 NAS).

To even bring up the topic of government necessitates acknowledgment that there are numerous versions of government within the body of Christ. If you're in a Presbyterian church, your government will be different than that of a Baptist church. You may be in a home church where there is no "recognized" government. You may be in a church that has apostolic government or one in which the pastor is the one who holds the responsibility to rule. There are local and translocal structures of government, which also operate differently. Although some are, in my opinion, better and closer to the scriptural pattern than others, the more important issue in this discussion is that God can and does rule through various forms of government, and He calls us to respect it.

The Christian who is humble and submitted to God will, however, recognize the value of submission to spiritual authority and look for legitimate spiritual authority to relate to in a proper way. The New Testament prophet should no longer be alone, standing outside of the religious order of the day, speaking judgment against it—as was so often the case in the Old Testament order. Rather, in collaboration with apostles, the prophet of today is part of the very foundation of the thing that God is trying to build, and is to be on the same team with pastors, teachers, and others. The real question we must ask ourselves is, "What are the motives and attitudes of our hearts?" Do we operate out of an attitude of rebellion, independence, and pride, or are we humble, teachable, and willing to be corrected?

It is important for those of you who minister prophetically to flow within the accepted protocol of the particular church or setting that you find yourself in. From church to church or group, there are various protocols set in place for various reasons. Often in home meetings, there will already be established relationships and much greater liberty. On the other hand, in some larger churches or conference settings, there will be the desire on the part of leadership for all prophetic ministry to be spoken into the public address system simply so that all may hear. Some churches have an open microphone for any and all "body ministry" to come forth. Some churches have a system of "clearing" words to be spoken through an established leader or authority.

Again, it is important to understand that most pastors or leaders are simply attempting to exercise their responsibility to guard their flock from unknown visitors who may or may not have a word that is appropriate for those he is responsible to lead. Usually, the larger the assembly, or the newer the individual is to a group, the more caution a leader will take in releasing public prophetic ministry. Find out the protocol of your particular setting and follow it.

Most aspiring prophesiers don't really understand a pastoral leader's sense of God-given stewardship and responsibility to protect the flock entrusted to them. They take seriously the fact that they will answer to God for what they allow into the assembly. What that creates for a leader is a continuous tension between passive and irresponsible latitude versus overt control. From situation to situation, group to group, and church to church, you will find protocol that represents every degree in between these two extremes in an attempt to walk in balance.

What most pastoral leaders know is that while prophetic ministry is a valuable "tool" for building the Kingdom, it also has potential for abuse and misuse. One of the dilemmas that every pastor or leader faces is the tension between "quality control" versus an "equipping" environment. It is no wonder that many well-meaning but misperceiving pastoral leaders are gun-shy when it comes to those who claim to speak on behalf of God as a prophet/prophetess. In my own circles, we jokingly refer to trainees as "Prophets-In-Training," or "P.I.T.'s," and sometimes the blunders made by trainees are the pits (pun intended).

Sphere

It is very important for each of us to discern and know our particular "sphere" of authorization. Paul knew, for instance, that he was an apostle to some but not to others. He knew his sphere. There are national prophetic voices like Paul Cain, Bill Hamon, Rick Joyner, Cindy Jacobs, etc., but there are few with that high a profile. Then there are thousands who have great effectiveness within their smaller sphere but are prophets nonetheless.

If you study the callings and portfolios of the Old Testament prophets, you discover that some are called to nations and some to one particular group, such as the tribe of Judah, etc. The extent of Jonah's prophetic ministry, for instance, was to one city. It is very common to find someone in a local church who is not recognized translocally, but is, in fact, very much a prophet "in house." It is somewhat limiting for us to hold to a view that only "full-time" or "translocal" ministries are the only ones who are prophets. That would have excluded Daniel, who was in political administration; Amos, who was a shepherd; or even David, who was a king. For instance, I have a businessman in the church I lead who is a very proficient prophetic voice in our midst, but he is not in "full-time ministry" and has rarely ministered outside our local church. But I view him as a prophet and value his ministry. I also have several persons whom I would be willing to call "in-house" prophetesses in our local church who also have no translocal ministry or "official position," but are very much prophetesses of the Lord. It is important to know your sphere so that you do not go beyond the grace God has given you.

Sphere and Content

Perhaps one of the biggest misconceptions people have regarding prophetic ministry is that it should be ministered in a judgmental, condemning, or rebuking way. Although prophets may speak of judgment, this is reserved for the mature who function in the office of the prophet and who are recognized as such in the body of Christ. First Corinthians 14:3 and 14:12 clarify that we should seek to edify, exhort, and comfort for the building up of the body of Christ.

Budding prophetic ministries can often fall into the trap of thinking they must come forth with some heavy word of direction or correction that will somehow lend credence to their position before God and men as a "heavy weight" in the spirit. The actual fact is that the Scripture clearly indicates the primary purpose of prophetic ministry is edification, exhortation, and comfort; in other words, to build up, stir up, and cheer up (see 1 Cor. 14).

Having been exposed to many substantial internationally recognized prophetic ministries who had no one to impress and nothing to prove, I have noticed that even they have the predominate amount of their ministry centered around edification, exhortation, and comfort. It is the unbroken and immature who seem most often to run to the opportunity to correct others. Does God ever call for someone to speak correction or direction? Of course, but again, it is more often when someone has come to the place where they have no one that they're trying to impress and nothing that they are trying to prove, that God can begin to use them to bring directive or corrective words to His precious body, His bride. The Scripture that Paul places right in the middle of his instruction about functioning in the gifts of the Spirit is vitally important to this issue:

> *If I have the gift of prophecy and can fathom all mysteries and all knowledge, and if I have a faith that can move mountains, but have not love, I am nothing* (1 Corinthians 13:2 NIV).

I'm not saying that established prophets and their message do not at times go quite beyond edification, exhortation, and comfort. Their prophetic ministry can reach into correction, direction, judgment, discipline, revelation, discernment of the body, and even creative initiative through the speaking of God-originated words (see Gen. 1).

The problem, however, with some of the so-called "prophetic" stuff accepted in some circles is that it is nothing more than arrogant, critical, faultfinding bitterness, wrapped in the cloak of the "lone, persecuted, truth-telling prophet." I like what I heard Pastor Loron Sandford (John and Paula's son) say one time: "Quite often prophets are persecuted not because of the content of their message, but rather that the prophet is being a turkey."

The problem is unless he/she is conformed to the image of Christ (as opposed to some Old Testament prophetic type), he/she will miss the heart of God, which is expressed *fully* and *completely* in Jesus—"the fullness of the Godhead [in] bodily [form]" (Col. 2:9). Jesus said, "If you've seen Me you've seen the Father" (see Jn. 14:9).

To be like Jesus means to be full of grace and truth. We need to communicate God's truth, but with His heart of love and grace. Of course, some would point to the case of Jesus driving the moneychangers from the temple as an excuse for anger or prophetic judgment. The faultiness behind that perception is a misunderstanding of what Jesus was doing at that time. What we actually see in that instance was Jesus the apostle in action, setting the house in order, rather than Jesus the prophet. The spokesman for God must always filter the "information" he/she wants to share "as from God" through the merciful and compassionate heart from which God would say it. This way we will stay safely within the bounds of proper prophetic ministry and will be used mightily of God to build what He wants built—a glorious church for His return. He wants the church built via relationship, not torn apart through offensive prophetic behavior.

> *So also you, since you are zealous of spiritual gifts, seek to abound for the edification of the church* (1 Corinthians 14:12 NAS).

For those who would prophesy but have not been given leadership responsibility or the responsibility to "steer" the meeting, avoid giving directive words to the congregation. God does sometimes bring directive prophecy through proven prophets. Although God may give a participant a word that would change the entire direction or flow of a service, the responsibility for that decision is ultimately given by God to the leadership—the operating government in any given setting—and should be channeled through them. The biggest difficulty arises from the fact that immature prophetic ministers can fall into the trap of attempting to control things through directive prophecy that is way beyond their sphere of authority to direct. God Himself has established other offices as well as the prophetic that also have responsibility to govern and direct. *Don't* be offended if your word is held back. (It might even be a test from God!)

It is very important to remain teachable. A teachable attitude is a reflection of humility, which pleases God. Always be willing to have a word judged. If the nature of the word is a personal prophecy, it is a good policy to have a witness with you or to in some way record what is spoken (using cassette recorders, writing out the words, etc.). This is a very clear principle from Scripture:

> *And let two or three prophets speak, and let the others pass judgment. ... For you can all prophesy one by one, so that all may learn and all may be exhorted; and the spirits of prophets are subject to prophets* (1 Corinthians 14:29,31-32 NAS).

It makes it a lot easier for a leader to risk letting someone speak if there is a willingness on the part of the prophesier to be corrected. After all, we *all* have blind spots.

Regarding itinerate ministries, the question is occasionally asked: "How much authority does a visiting prophetic ministry have to bring correction or direction to a local church?" The answer is very simply: "As much as he or she is invited to have." Just because someone is a prophet does not automatically mean that he or she can usurp another's legitimate governmental sphere. Government and prophetic ministry are two different ministries. This is not to say that someone may not exercise ministry in both areas at the same time. As a visiting ministry, it is important to understand what sphere of authority you've been given.

Scripture tells us that anyone who receives a prophet in the name of a prophet receives a prophet's reward. That is, they receive the ministry that the prophet brings. On the other hand, if they do not receive a prophet as a prophet, then you are not a prophet...*to them!* So, in such circumstances, it is wise not to try to be. If a prophetic ministry is received by a local church leadership to minister to their group, that ministry should come as a servant with the purpose of supporting that local leadership. The proper attitude would be that of one who comes submitted to the authority and government in that place.

Of course, if a prophet comes, who also has been given translocal governmental oversight to that group, the authority issue changes dramatically. If you have been given a recognized position of authority translocally, then your ministry will be different than one who is coming from outside by invitation of the local authority. Paul the apostle knew that he was an apostle to some but not to others. He exercised translocal authority in the case of the church in Corinth, but demonstrated a yielding to the government in Jerusalem when he visited the apostles there.

Addendum to Pastors

As a prophetic equipper myself, and as a leader of a very prophetically gifted congregation, I have encouraged the folks to "risk" and move out (according to their proportion of faith). At the same time, the people all know that our church is an equipping environment; meaning, the people know that they have a responsibility to discern for themselves if the word was "right on" or not.

But solid food is for the mature, who because of practice have their senses trained to discern good and evil (Hebrews 5:14 NAS).

In my experience, one of the best means of growing in discernment and "practicing" is by being exposed to accurate and inaccurate words. The best defense against counterfeit or sub-par ministry in the prophetic is to have the genuine to compare it with. The trouble is, most of the time, a valid budding prophetic ministry will give words that are not either perfectly accurate or dramatically off. (For instance, it might be 80 percent divine inspiration and 20 percent our own added commentary and opinions.)

We place a high value on body ministry and the operation of the gifts and deliberately cultivate an "equipping," or training, environment (see 1 Cor. 14:26-33). Therefore, our church is more tolerant than most. We also have some very strong and seasoned prophets/prophetesses in our midst, so it is easy for the members to differentiate between the "right on" words and the flaky stuff. (Oh yes, if you allow liberty for the gifts to flow, you *will* get flaky stuff!) And they also have a commitment from me that if a word is too far out—such as doctrinally in error or wrongly directive—I will kindly, but very definitely, bring correction to it.

Our people know that I grant great liberty for any exhortations, words, testimonies, etc., in the assembly, but that I will not hesitate to correct a word, as well, if it is doctrinally errant or if there is some other problem associated with it. (I have had to do that *very rarely*, but the folks know I will, if it is needed.) The fact that the people know that I will graciously correct a word if need be gives them great security, and, in fact, it creates even more willingness for them to "risk" and step out.

We also put a value on the preservation of the word of the Lord, so we try as often as possible to get it taped. Therefore, such words must come through a microphone and must flow with what else is going on. Also, the worship leaders deliberately "make room" for prophetic ministry to come forth. This, of course, makes it simply a practical necessity for those with a word to share to step up to a microphone and wait for an appropriate opening. Home groups contain a different dynamic, of course, though we are not addressing that protocol here.

While on the subject of taping, I'll add this: We discourage "parking lot" prophecies. That is, if you have a word for someone, it should be done in the open assembly or at least be open to inspection (e.g., have witnesses, tape it, have it written down, or something). This goes a long way toward protecting the flock from unscrupulous manipulators who would try to control through prophecy for any personal gain.

God has given the gifts to the church for the building up of the church. As we allow the tools He Himself provided, we will see the building built stronger and faster, and we will be used mightily of God to build what He wants built—that is, a glorious church awaiting His return.

Section IV

The Foundation at Work

And coming to Him as to a living stone, rejected by men, but choice and precious in the sight of God, you also, as living stones, are being built up as a spiritual house for a holy priesthood, to offer up spiritual sacrifices acceptable to God through Jesus Christ (1 Peter 2:4-5 NAS).

Chapter 12

The House of David:
The Government Restored

The apostles were baffled. This thing called "the church" was expanding in a way they had not foreseen. They had just received reports from Paul and Barnabas of Gentiles coming to God by faith and receiving the Holy Spirit, just as they had. Then "senior apostle" James remembered a particular prophecy. His statement is recorded in Acts 15:13-18:

> *And after they had become silent, James answered, saying, "Men and brethren, listen to me: Simon has declared how God at the first visited the Gentiles to take out of them a people for His name. And with this the words of the prophets agree, just as it is written: 'After this I will return and will rebuild the tabernacle of David, which has fallen down; I will rebuild its ruins, and I will set it up; so that the rest of mankind may seek the Lord, even all the Gentiles who are called by My name, says the Lord who does all these things.' Known to God from eternity are all His works."*

The tabernacle of David, known of and planned by God from eternity past, was now beginning to be rebuilt. But what exactly is this "house" that God said He Himself would rebuild in the last days?

In the days of King David's dominion, righteousness ruled out of Zion. God was pleased with David because of his devotion to the Lord and his desire to worship Him. David loved the presence of God, and God loved that about David. In David's zeal to worship before the presence of

God, he housed the ark of the covenant in an open tent and conscripted a 24-hour choral and instrumental ensemble to offer up continuous praises to the Lord. In fact, throughout history since the time of David, his manner of worship was the pattern to which the people of God returned whenever there was a return to God.

But David did not only pioneer the manner of corporate worship that would set the pattern for worship before God's presence forever; he also exhibited a dominion of righteousness. David's rule on earth represented God's rule through man. A restoration of David's fallen tabernacle is not only a return to worship, but it is a return to God's rule among men. Although David is known as a prophet, he can also be viewed as a type of apostolic government through his service as a righteous king. The house of David, in fact, is destined to rule forever throughout eternity.

As it happened, sometime after David set up the tent of God's presence, where the ark of the covenant was housed, he had the bright idea to propose to God that he build Him a house. God must have laughed. He explained to David that He didn't need a physical house in which to dwell and that He could not be contained within a physical building anyway; but just because of David's attitude, He promised that He would build him a "house" that would last forever. This house would be a place from which a descendant of David would rule forever. The significance of this house is much greater than most realize, as it pertains to the characteristics, dominion, and commission of the last-days church.

The promises God gave to David pertaining to this "house" are recorded in Second Samuel 7.

> *"Wherever I have moved about with all the children of Israel, have I ever spoken a word to anyone from the tribes of Israel, whom I commanded to shepherd My people Israel, saying, 'Why have you not built Me a house of cedar?'" Now therefore, thus shall you say to My servant David, "Thus says the Lord of hosts: 'I took you from the sheepfold, from following the sheep, to be ruler over My people, over Israel. And I have been with you wherever you have gone, and have cut off all your enemies from before you, and have made you a great name, like the name of the great men who are on the earth. Moreover I will appoint a place for My people Israel, and will plant them, that they may dwell in a place of their own and move no more; nor shall the sons of wickedness oppress them anymore, as previously, since the time that I commanded judges to be over My people Israel, and have caused you to rest from all your enemies. Also the Lord tells you that He will make you a house. When your days are fulfilled and you rest*

with your fathers, I will set up your seed after you, who will come from your body, and I will establish his kingdom. He shall build a house for My name, and I will establish the throne of his kingdom forever. ... And your house and your kingdom shall be established forever before you. Your throne shall be established forever' " (2 Samuel 7:7-13,16).

To see what happened next shows us insight into the covenant-keeping nature of God. It was only one generation later that Solomon did evil in the sight of the Lord, and yet for His servant David's sake, He kept His word.

Therefore the Lord said to Solomon, "Because you have done this, and have not kept My covenant and My statutes, which I have commanded you, I will surely tear the kingdom away from you and give it to your servant. Nevertheless I will not do it in your days, for the sake of your father David; I will tear it out of the hand of your son. However I will not tear away the whole kingdom; I will give one tribe to your son for the sake of my servant David, and for the sake of Jerusalem which I have chosen" (1 Kings 11:11-13).

About 85 years after David, we again see God's commitment to His covenant with bad King Abijam:

And he walked in all the sins of his father, which he had done before him; his heart was not loyal to the Lord his God, as was the heart of his father David. Nevertheless for David's sake the Lord his God gave him a lamp in Jerusalem, by setting up his son after him and by establishing Jerusalem (1 Kings 15:3-4).

During the reign of good King Hezekiah, 313 years later, deliverance came once again as God speaks from the mouth of His prophet Isaiah:

"For out of Jerusalem shall go a remnant, and those who escape from Mount Zion. The zeal of the Lord of hosts will do this." Therefore thus says the Lord concerning the king of Assyria: "He shall not come into this city, nor shoot an arrow there, nor come before it with shield, nor build a siege mound against it. By the way that he came, by the same shall he return; and he shall not come into this city," says the Lord. "For I will defend this city, to save it for My own sake and for My servant David's sake" (2 Kings 19:31-34).

God intends to keep His covenant. In fact, the rule of the house of David is again expanded upon and defined by prophet Isaiah in Isaiah 16:5: "In mercy the throne will be established; and One will sit on it in truth, in the tabernacle of David, judging and seeking justice and hastening righteousness." We see here that mercy, truth, justice, and righteousness are components of this dominion.

Years later, when things could not seem to be any worse, the prophet Amos arose and spoke this prophetic promise:

> *"On that day I will raise up the tabernacle of David, which has fallen down, and repair its damages; I will raise up its ruins, and rebuild it as in the days of old; that they may possess the remnant of Edom, and all the Gentiles who are called by My name," says the Lord who does this thing* (Amos 9:11-12).

This clearly tied the reestablished rule of the house of David with the worldwide declaration of the Kingdom of God. This Amos prophecy was the Scripture quoted by James at the council in Jerusalem and is a key Scripture in understanding God's end-time plans for the house of David, which is the church; for we now see Jesus, the Son of David, who became the Cornerstone of the house and the builder of an eternal house that is now called "the church."

We see this "house" described in several sections of New Testament Scripture. Paul described it in his letter to the Ephesians.

> *Now, therefore, you are no longer strangers and foreigners, but fellow citizens with the saints and members of the household of God, having been built on the foundation of the apostles and prophets, Jesus Christ Himself being the chief cornerstone, in whom the whole building, being fitted together, grows into a holy temple in the Lord, in whom you also are being built together for a dwelling place of God in the Spirit* (Ephesians 2:19-22).

Peter described it in his first Epistle as well and shows us one of its significant purposes: the offering of spiritual sacrifices to God.

> *Coming to Him as to a living stone, rejected indeed by men, but chosen by God and precious, you also, as living stones, are being built up a spiritual house, a holy priesthood, to offer up spiritual sacrifices acceptable to God through Jesus Christ. Therefore it is also contained in the Scripture, "Behold, I lay in Zion a chief cornerstone, elect, precious, and he who believes on Him will by no means be put to shame"* (1 Peter 2:4-6).

We are the house of God. We are the tabernacle being restored. We have become the expression of Kingdom dominion after the order of David, a "nation of kings and priests" through our great God and Savior, none other than Jesus of Nazareth, Son of David.

Jesus said that He would build His church, and nothing would prevail against it (see Mt. 16:18). *That* is the tabernacle of David.

Worship, But More Than Worship

We must see this "house" as something much bigger than just a group of folks who get together on occasion and sing some songs and do a religious routine. We have become a temple in the Lord, a dwelling place of God in the Spirit, a spiritual house to offer up spiritual sacrifices that are acceptable to God through Jesus Christ. Wherever there is true worship, we also see a release of a dimension of authority that is characteristic of the apostolic. We literally take on, and to an extent become, an expression of God's rule upon the earth.

This pattern and progression is seen in the ministry of Jesus when He came into the temple surrounded by pure and true worship. We have touched on this event several times throughout this book, but now let's take a deeper look. The setting is described in Matthew 20 and 21.

There was a very loud procession as Jesus traveled the distance between Jericho and Jerusalem that day. Many people felt the prophetic significance of the moment, and some even began to cry out, "Have mercy on us, O Lord, Son of David!" (Mt. 20:30) As He drew closer to the city, riding on a donkey, the multitudes began to cry out, "Hosanna to the Son of David! 'Blessed is He who comes in the name of the Lord!' Hosanna in the highest!" (Mt. 21:9)

Note these things associated with Jesus' being acknowledged as the Son of David. They knew David's house was to someday be restored. The crowds were undoubtedly wondering, *Could this be the one?* But then we see a side of Jesus not often observed. As He came into His temple full of the authority of God, He began to set the house in order.

> *Then Jesus went into the temple of God and drove out all those who bought and sold in the temple, and overturned the tables of the money changers and the seats of those who sold doves. And He said to them, "It is written, 'My house shall be called a house of prayer,' but you have made it a 'den of thieves.'" Then the blind and the lame came to Him in the temple, and He healed them. But when the chief priests and scribes saw the wonderful things that He did, and the children crying out in the temple and saying, "Hosanna to the Son of David!" they were indignant and said to Him, "Do You hear what these are saying?" And Jesus said to them, "Yes. Have you never read, 'Out of the mouth of babes and nursing infants You have perfected praise'?"* (Matthew 21:12-16)

He had been there many times before, but now there was something different. Now He was moving in his apostolic mantle. He was sent from God, with the authority of God. He came in an atmosphere of perfected praise, and He came cleansing the temple, calling for prayer, and healing the sick.

Restored dimensions of worship release restored dimensions of authority, out of which apostolic order is released on the earth. There is a level of restored apostolic power that will only be released as these two things come forth together.

It is very important, however, to recognize the attributes of the rule of God. As almost a parallel to the study of the Kingdom authority within the Davidic covenant, we see a commitment from God to show forth what Scriptures call the "sure mercies of David" as a part of this covenant (see Is. 55:3). Isaiah 16:5 states, "In mercy the throne will be established; and One will sit on it in truth, in the tabernacle of David, judging and seeking justice and hastening righteousness." Here we see that His throne is established in mercy. Later, we will look at the other principle, that His throne is also established in righteousness.

His Throne Established in Mercy—The Sure Mercies of David

In Paul's dramatic sermon recorded in Acts 13, he stated:

We tell you the good news: What God promised our fathers He has fulfilled for us, their children, by raising up Jesus. As it is written in the second Psalm: "You are My Son; today I have become Your Father." The fact that God raised him from the dead, never to decay, is stated in these words: "I will give you the holy and sure blessings promised to David" (Acts 13:32-34 NIV).

We see here that through Jesus we have become partakers of the sure mercies or the covenantal mercies of David. The sure mercies of God are simply the steadfast intentions of God to do us good. We must know that God is a God of compassion and mercy.

Therefore know that the Lord your God, He is God, the faithful God who keeps covenant and mercy for a thousand generations with those who love Him and keep His commandments (Deuteronomy 7:9).

"For a mere moment I have forsaken you, but with great mercies I will gather you. With a little wrath I hid My face from you for a moment; but with everlasting kindness I will have mercy on you," says the Lord, your Redeemer (Isaiah 54:7-8).

This I recall to my mind, therefore I have hope. Through the Lord's mercies we are not consumed, because His compassions fail not. They are new every morning; great is Your faithfulness (Lamentations 3:21-23).

In addition to the writers above, David also knew of the mercies of God, the steadfast intentions of God to do him good. The following is an abbreviated survey of psalms that reveal David's insights into the mercy of God.

> *Many sorrows shall be to the wicked; but he who trusts in the Lord, mercy shall surround him. Be glad in the Lord and rejoice, you righteous; and shout for joy, all you upright in heart!* (Psalm 32:10-11)

> *But You, O Lord, are a God full of compassion, and gracious, long-suffering and abundant in mercy and truth* (Psalm 86:15).

> *Enter into His gates with thanksgiving, and into His courts with praise. Be thankful to Him, and bless His name. For the Lord is good; His mercy is everlasting, and His truth endures to all generations* (Psalm 100:4-5).

> *The Lord is merciful and gracious, slow to anger, and abounding in mercy. He will not always strive with us, nor will He keep His anger forever. He has not dealt with us according to our sins, nor punished us according to our iniquities. For as the heavens are high above the earth, so great is His mercy toward those who fear Him* (Psalm 103:8-11).

> *But the mercy of the Lord is from everlasting to everlasting on those who fear Him, and His righteousness to children's children* (Psalm 103:17).

> *Oh, give thanks to the Lord, for He is good! For His mercy endures forever. Oh, give thanks to the God of gods! For His mercy endures forever. Oh, give thanks to the Lord of lords! For His mercy endures forever* (Psalm 136:1-3).

> *The Lord takes pleasure in those who fear Him, in those who hope in His mercy* (Psalm 147:11).

The prophet Isaiah prophesied of the sure mercies of David and that we are partakers.

> *Ho! Everyone who thirsts, come to the waters; and you who have no money, come, buy and eat. Yes, come, buy wine and milk without money and without price. Why do you spend money for what is not bread, and your wages for what does not satisfy? Listen carefully to Me, and eat what is good, and let your soul delight itself in abundance. Incline your ear, and come to Me. Hear, and your soul shall*

*live; and I will make an everlasting covenant with you—the sure mer-
cies of David. ... Let the wicked forsake his way, and the unrighteous
man his thoughts; let him return to the Lord, and He will have mercy
on him; and to our God, for He will abundantly pardon* (Isaiah
55:1-3,7).

The dominion of God is a Kingdom of mercy. His rule is full of
mercy for those who come to Him in faith. His rule is also established in
righteousness. Although these may seem to be opposing concepts, we
must see that the cross of Jesus God established both righteousness and
mercy. He found a way around His just judgment to show us His mercy
and grace. The next chapter addresses the rule of righteousness.

Chapter 13

Mount Zion–The City of God

Government in Zion

David established his rulership out of Jerusalem, a city on the top of Mount Zion. The Scriptures refer to Mount Zion and the city of Jerusalem as a picture of the government of God. Psalm 2:6 prophetically decreed in reference to Jesus: "Yet I have set My King on My holy hill of Zion." The picture is carried forward in Isaiah's prophecy to show the eventual, total dominion of the Kingdom of God over all other kingdoms and dominions.

> *Now it shall come to pass in the latter days that the mountain of the Lord's house shall be established on the top of the mountains, and shall be exalted above the hills; and all nations shall flow to it. Many people shall come and say, "Come, and let us go up to the mountain of the Lord, to the house of the God of Jacob; He will teach us His ways, and we shall walk in His paths." For out of Zion shall go forth the law, and the word of the Lord from Jerusalem* (Isaiah 2:2-3).

We know this is a direct reference to the Kingdom of God and His agency, the church, through what is stated in Hebrews 12:22-23:

> *But you have come to Mount Zion and to the city of the living God, the heavenly Jerusalem, to an innumerable company of angels, to the general assembly and church of the firstborn who are registered*

in heaven, to God the Judge of all, to the spirits of just men made perfect.

We, the church, are that city of which Matthew 5:14 states, "You are the light of the world. A city that is set on a hill cannot be hidden."

For those of us who have grown up in a western democratic form of government, rather than one of kings and kingdoms, the term *kingdom* can easily lose its simple significance. For me, the interposing of the word *government* for *kingdom* puts it into a much clearer perspective. In other words, the Kingdom of God is the government of God. It is the domain in which the King rules, or to say it another way, it is wherever Jesus is Lord.

Daniel saw and described it like this:

> *I was watching in the night visions, and behold, One like the Son of Man, coming with the clouds of heaven! He came to the Ancient of Days, and they brought Him near before Him. Then to Him was given dominion and glory and a kingdom, that all peoples, nations, and languages should serve Him. His dominion is an everlasting dominion, which shall not pass away, and His kingdom the one which shall not be destroyed* (Daniel 7:13-14).

At His ascension, Jesus said, "All authority has been given to Me in heaven and on earth" (Mt. 28:18b). The rule of Jesus extends over all. He rules over space. He rules over time and eternity. He rules over nature, and His rule shall eventually and inevitably extend to every individual, for Scripture states in Philippians 2:10-11, "...at the name of Jesus every knee should bow...and that every tongue should confess that Jesus Christ is Lord, to the glory of God the Father."

Jesus demonstrated His Lordship—His rulership over creation—by turning water to wine, multiplying bread and fish, and even using His authority over the elements. He commanded the wind and waves; He exerted authority over demons and the domain of darkness, sickness, and disease, etc.

Where Jesus rules, demons flee, sickness is healed, and captives are set free. It is interesting that over and over again when Jesus and the gospel of the Kingdom are mentioned together in Scripture, those things were happening. And, of course, there are many other characteristics of His reign besides power and authority over the works of darkness, such as righteousness, peace, and joy.

But although He rules sovereignly over all His creation, there remains one domain that, for a time, has eluded His Lordship, and that has been only by sovereign permission. That domain is the heart and volition of man, including the "world system" created by man that man, in turn, betrayed to the evil one.

The Scripture, however, also indicates that through His coming, Jesus bought back that one last, lost domain, and thus was established as Lord of all, once and for all, which now gives us the conclusion of the matter. He is Lord of all! He rules out of Zion. But His Kingdom has also been likened to leaven, which slowly and subtly invades and infiltrates the entire loaf of bread.

The Kingdom is come, wherever Jesus is given rule, and that rule is eventual and inevitable. That is why, when Jesus becomes Lord of our lives, the Kingdom also comes to our lives. Where Jesus is Lord in the church, the Kingdom of God has come to the church. Where Jesus is Lord of our eating habits, our financial dealings, our relationships, *there* the Kingdom has come. His Kingdom is inevitable. We are all destined to acknowledge it by the confession of our tongue and the bending of our knee. The fact is, everyone *will* acknowledge Him as Lord. The choice each one has is to do so willingly now, for which there is great benefit, or under duress later at the final judgment. Nevertheless, He is Lord! Glory to the *King*!

The Scepter of Righteousness

In the previous chapter we looked at the fact that His throne is established in mercy; yet it is also established in righteousness.

> *Your throne, O God, is forever and ever; a scepter of righteousness is the scepter of Your kingdom. You love righteousness and hate wicked-ness...* (Psalm 45:6-7).

A scepter is an ornate rod or wand that serves as an emblem of regal or imperial power and authority in the hand of a ruler. The scepter in the king's hand represents his authority and dominion. We are told in the above Scripture that God's scepter is a scepter of righteousness. That is, His authority is righteousness. It could also be said that the authority of righteousness is the authority of His Kingdom. So the extension of His rule is the extension of His righteousness. In fact, His Kingdom is described as a Kingdom of righteousness, peace, and joy in the Holy Spirit (see Rom. 14:17). Add that to the fact that God wants to extend *His* rule and *His* dominion through His people, and we see that it is through righteousness that we have dominion. Therefore, as we reflect His righteousness, we express His dominion. Put more simply, our level of righteousness determines our level of dominion. It is through righteousness that we have rule in life.

Of course, we must first understand that we are not talking about the righteousness by which we are saved. That is an imputed righteousness given to us as a gift and received by faith. There is, however, a righteousness manifested when we walk out the righteousness that has been provided for us. God desires for us to not only receive a "positional righteousness" (i.e., right standing in His eyes), but also a practical experience of *being* righteous.

It is this latter righteousness that determines our level of rule and dominion in life. It is the righteousness that comes as we choose to walk in the empowering grace that He has provided. It is our destiny and purpose to be extensions of God's rule in the earth. Ephesians 1:22-23 tells us that we are to be His body, the fullness of Him that fills all in all. He wants to restore to us the dominion betrayed to the devil at the fall of man and grant us to reign in life in Christ Jesus. We are meant to be extensions of His righteous rule. We are called to advance His Kingdom. The Kingdom of God is simply the domain of the King. It has come wherever Jesus is ruling.

To talk about government and authority, however, I must clarify that I am not attempting to define a natural form of church government. As stated before, the topic of ecclesiastical government is beyond the intentions of this book. What is important to understand is that true apostolic government is expressed through the authority of God in the realm of the Spirit. Although the emergence of true spiritual authority will have a profound effect on the way church government operates, the primary point to be made here is that a truly apostolic church is a church that understands the place it has to express dominion over darkness.

The Source of Authority

The point of all this is that we must see that there is authority in righteousness. Righteousness gives us dominion. Unrighteousness robs us of dominion. Let us arise and go forth in righteousness, full of the authority of God Himself to press back the domain of darkness and usher in the Kingdom of God.

Wherever He went, Jesus demonstrated what this would look like as He declared that the Kingdom is at hand, healed the sick, preached the gospel, and set the captives free.

> *...God anointed Jesus of Nazareth with the Holy Spirit and with power, who went about doing good and healing all who were oppressed by the devil, for God was with Him* (Acts 10:38).

He did this as one who was anointed with the Holy Spirit and power. Jesus received His anointing and commissioning to do the supernatural works He did from the Father.

> Then Jesus, being filled with the Holy Spirit, returned from the Jordan and was led by the Spirit into the wilderness (Luke 4:1).

> And Jesus returned in the power of the Spirit into Galilee: and a fame went out concerning Him through all the region round about (Luke 4:14 ASV).

We all love to read about the powerful and wonderful things Jesus did, as He opened blind eyes, healed the maimed and crippled, bound up the broken, gave people the good news of their sins being forgiven, etc. But when it comes to today, we often say, "Well, that is what Jesus did, but I'm not Jesus." That is true; we are not Jesus, but Jesus expects us to do the same things in the same way that He did. At the end of His earthly ministry, He said that He wanted us to continue with the same ministry (see Mt. 28:19-20). In fact, He said that the same anointing and commissioning He received from the Father He now imparts to us.

> So Jesus said to them again, "Peace to you! As the Father has sent Me, I also send you" (John 20:21).

In fact, He not only expects us to move in the same anointing and commissioning; He promised that we would do even greater things than He did. John 14:12 (NAS) states, "Truly, truly, I say to you, he who believes in Me, the works that I do shall he do also; and greater works than these shall he do; because I go to the Father."

In addition to that, Mark 16:17 (ASV) states, "And these signs shall accompany them that believe: in My name shall they cast out demons; they shall speak with new tongues."

The conclusion we must come to is that God wants to allow us to demonstrate His love and power in the same way Jesus did, and He has given His promise that we can move in the miraculous, even as He did. There is a world out there waiting to see the church move, not only in a proclamation, but also in a demonstration of the Spirit and power so that their faith would rest not in merely the wisdom of man but in the power of God.

The apostle Paul stated, "For the kingdom of God is not in word but in power" (1 Cor. 4:20). He also stated in First Thessalonians 1:5, "For our gospel did not come to you in word only, but also in power, and in the Holy Spirit and in much assurance...." Paul modeled how we should minister by the power of the Spirit.

And my speech and my preaching were not with persuasive words of human wisdom, but in demonstration of the Spirit and of power, that your faith should not be in the wisdom of men but in the power of God (1 Corinthians 2:4-5).

He even warned in Second Timothy 3:1-5 against those who have a form of godliness but deny its power:

But know this, that in the last days perilous times will come: for men will be lovers of themselves, lovers of money, boasters, proud, blasphemers, disobedient to parents, unthankful, unholy, unloving, unforgiving, slanderers, without self-control, brutal, despisers of good, traitors, headstrong, haughty, lovers of pleasure rather than lovers of God, having a form of godliness but denying its power. And from such people turn away!

The Kingdom we belong to is a Kingdom of power. We need to understand this power—where it comes from, what its purpose is, what it supplies to us, and who can wield it.

The source of power is God:

"But that you may know that the Son of Man has power on earth to forgive sins"–then He said to the paralytic, "Arise, take up your bed, and go to your house." And he arose and departed to his house. Now when the multitudes saw it, they marveled and glorified God, who had given such power to men (Matthew 9:6-8).

...His divine power has given to us all things that pertain to life and godliness (2 Peter 1:3a).

Finally, my brethren, be strong in the Lord and in the power of His might (Ephesians 6:10).

The purpose of power is to do good:

God anointed Jesus of Nazareth with the Holy Spirit and with power who went about doing good and healing all who were oppressed by the devil... (Acts 10:38).

His power saves us:

For I am not ashamed of the gospel of Christ, for it is the power of God to salvation for everyone who believes... (Romans 1:16).

For the message of the cross is foolishness to those who are perishing, but to us who are being saved it is the power of God (1 Corinthians 1:18).

His power heals us:

...And the power of the Lord was present to heal them (Luke 5:17).

And the whole multitude sought to touch Him, for power went out from Him and healed them all (Luke 6:19).

His power delivers us:

Then they were all amazed and spoke among themselves, saying, "What a word this is! For with authority and power He commands the unclean spirits, and they come out" (Luke 4:36).

His power produces fresh hope:

Now may the God of hope fill you with all joy and peace in believing, that you may abound in hope by the power of the Holy Spirit (Romans 15:13).

His power keeps us:

Blessed be the God...who according to His abundant mercy has begotten us again to a living hope...reserved in heaven for you, who are kept by the power of God through faith for salvation ready to be revealed in the last time (1 Peter 1:3-5).

He wants us to wield His power to press back the kingdom of darkness.

"Behold, I give you the authority to trample on serpents and scorpions, and over all the power of the enemy, and nothing shall by any means hurt you" (Luke 10:19).

"Behold, I send the Promise of My Father upon you; but tarry in the city of Jerusalem until you are endued with power from on high" (Luke 24:49).

"But you shall receive power when the Holy Spirit has come upon you; and you shall be witnesses to Me...to the end of the earth" (Acts 1:8).

But we have this treasure in earthen vessels, that the excellence of the power may be of God and not of us (2 Corinthians 4:7).

The eyes of your understanding being enlightened; that you may know what is the hope of His calling, what are the riches of the glory of His inheritance in the saints, and what is the exceeding greatness of His power toward us who believe, according to the working of His mighty power which He worked in Christ when He raised Him from the dead and seated Him at His right hand in the heavenly places (Ephesians 1:18-20).

Now to Him who is able to do exceedingly abundantly above all that we ask or think, according to the power that works in us, to Him be glory in the church by Christ Jesus to all generations, forever and ever. Amen (Ephesians 3:20-21).

Drawing the Battle Lines

In spiritual warfare, we are literally entering into the conflict of two kingdoms—the Kingdom of God and the kingdom of darkness. Our task is to bring the power and purpose of God to bear against the power and purpose of the enemy. In every area of life, there is a will and purpose from God against which the enemy schemes relentlessly, trying to thwart God's redemptive work on the earth. The ultimate triumph of God's Kingdom is a foregone conclusion; that issue was settled once and for all on Calvary. The salvation God has provided through the cross of Christ is thorough. It has provided everything we need for life and godliness. So why does it seem, at times, that provision isn't being realized in our lives?

To answer that question, we need to understand something about the nature of our battle. We need to understand that, although the Kingdom of God has claimed legal right of redemption, delivering mankind and the earth itself from every curse, our enemy is a squatter who only reluctantly leaves at our insistence, yet who knows that he must go if we insist. The problem is that most often we don't know the extensive implications of God's redemptive work, nor the powerful tools and weapons that He has put in our hands to bring this redemption to bear against the enemy. We don't understand that He has commissioned us to be instruments of His dominion.

The primary way we accomplish this is through prayer. It is by prayer that we experience the breakthrough of God's redemptive purpose into mankind's affairs. It is by prayer that we enforce the authority of Heaven on earth. By prayer, we literally cooperate with God to bring His dominion to bear against whatever is contrary to it. Prayer is most often the missing ingredient that will move us beyond the realm of natural strength into the realm of the supernatural power of God. Is it any wonder, then, that the enemy will do anything he can to keep us from prayer or that he runs scared when God's people find their place at the throne of grace and begin to pray in earnest?

We must understand that our job is to persist in our prayers against the kingdom of darkness, to relentlessly proclaim, "Thy Kingdom come, Thy will be done" (see Mt. 6:10). If we see our prayers as weapons against the powers of darkness, we will begin to realize how important it is to persist in prayer and insist that God's will be done. We then become instruments of His dominion in the earth. So, let us be in prayer at all times in the spirit with all manner of prayer and entreaty (see Eph. 6:18). To that end, keep alert and watch with strong purpose and perseverance, interceding on behalf of all the saints and pressing back the domain of darkness until God's Kingdom has complete preeminence.

Chapter 14

Prophetic Destiny and Apostolic Reformation

The setting was during one of the lowest points in Israel's history. King Manasseh had already been in power for 50 years, during which time he had led Judah into the worse condition of paganism and idol worship that they had ever experienced. Not only did he do all manner of evil that the Lord called an abomination in His sight, he also led Judah into all manner of sin, including child sacrifice, witchcraft, divination, as well as sexually perverse idol worship (see 2 Kings 21).

At this point, his 16-year-old son, Amon, fathered a child and named him Josiah. Amon went on to become the king six years later when his father died, but he, too, did evil in the sight of the Lord and was killed just two years later, leaving Josiah king of Judah at the tender age of eight years old.

Into this wicked culture came Josiah, who typically would have followed in the footsteps of his father and his grandfather, but God had a prophetic destiny that included Josiah. In fact, Josiah's kingship had been prophesied by name almost 300 years earlier, and it was said of him that he would be a great reformer (see 1 Kings 13:1-3).

At the age of 16, Josiah began to radically seek the Lord after the manner of his ancestor King David (see 2 Chron. 34:3), and David's manner of seeking God was total commitment. Note his words in Psalm 63:1-2:

O God, You are my God; early will I seek You; my soul thirsts for You; my flesh longs for You in a dry and thirsty land where there is no water. So I have looked for You in the sanctuary, to see Your power and Your glory.

Because of this very zeal for God that David displayed and because of his desire to see the house of God built, God had made a covenant with David that his house would stand forever. Josiah found himself being born along and serving the purposes of God in his generation, according to God's covenant promises to David. The zeal for God's house is the backbone of apostolic reformation.

Josiah went against the tide of the popular culture of his day, became one of the great kings of Judah, and engineered a major reformation in his generation. He also stands as an example to the youth of our day. God is raising a generation that will serve the Lord from their youth.

There are several keys to reformation that we can learn from the reign of Josiah and the reformation that he brought to the nation; but before we look at them, we must understand that the body of Christ has arrived at a similar time in God's prophetic purposes. God has ordained that this is a time for apostolic reformation. In the midst of wickedness on every side, He has a chosen people prepared with a prophetic destiny who will arise and become instruments of reformation.

We have arrived at a new day in God's eternal purposes. We are in the time of the restoration of all things spoken by the prophets of old (see Acts 3:19-21). He has said that He would again restore the house of David that had fallen down as was prophesied by Amos:

On that day I will raise up the tabernacle of David, which has fallen down, and repair its damages; I will raise up its ruins, and rebuild it as in the days of old (Amos 9:11).

This is "that day."

He has His prepared vessels who are rising to the task and will see the plans of God through to the perfecting of a glorious church—a spotless bride—in preparation for His return. These are people of faith, who have confidence in the Holy Spirit's ability to do what He intends to do, which is to prepare the bride for the Bridegroom. I really don't think that Jesus is coming back for a shriveled-up, emaciated bride to whom He will have to administer mouth-to-mouth resuscitation as they make their way up to Heaven. I think He will have a bride who is prepared and glorious.

I guess it can be a matter of which Scriptures you focus on. For instance, there are many Scriptures that show a wicked culture, ripe for judgment at the end of the age (e.g., 2 Tim. 3:1-5), but there are also many that show us a victorious eschatology for the church at the end of the age. Here are a few:

> *Husbands, love your wives, just as Christ also loved the church and gave Himself for her, that He might sanctify and cleanse her with the washing of water by the word, that He might present her to Himself a glorious church, not having spot or wrinkle or any such thing, but that she should be holy and without blemish. ... This is a great mystery, but I speak concerning Christ and the church* (Ephesians 5:25-27, 32; see also Revelation 21:2,9-11).

Take note of the conditional terms in the following Scriptures:

> *But those things which God foretold by the mouth of all His prophets, that the Christ would suffer, He has thus fulfilled. Repent therefore and be converted, that your sins may be blotted out, so that times of refreshing may come from the presence of the Lord, and that He may send Jesus Christ, who was preached to you before, whom heaven must receive until the times of restoration of all things, which God has spoken by the mouth of all His holy prophets since the world began* (Acts 3:18-21).

> *And He Himself gave some to be apostles, some prophets, some evangelists, and some pastors and teachers, for the equipping of the saints for the work of ministry, for the edifying of the body of Christ,* **till** *we all come to the unity of the faith and of the knowledge of the Son of God, to a perfect man, to the measure of the stature of the fullness of Christ; that we should no longer be children, tossed to and fro and carried about with every wind of doctrine, by the trickery of men, in the cunning craftiness of deceitful plotting, but, speaking the truth in love, may grow up in all things into Him who is the head—Christ—from whom the whole body, joined and knit together by what every joint supplies, according to the effective working by which every part does its share, causes growth of the body for the edifying of itself in love* (Ephesians 4:11-16).

Then, of course, there is Jesus' prayer in John 17 that I personally believe will come to pass. (Sometimes we may wonder how it will happen, but since Jesus prayed it, I believe it will happen.)

> *I do not pray for these alone, but also for those who will believe in Me through their word; that they all may be one, as You, Father, are in Me, and I in You; that they also may be one in Us, that the world may believe that You sent Me. And the glory which You gave Me I have given them, that they may be one just as We are one: I in them, and*

You in Me; that they may be made perfect in one, and that the world may know that You have sent Me, and have loved them as You have loved Me (John 17:20-23).

Sounds pretty good to me.

There are a number of implications with regard to becoming an apostolic church. But first of all, we must be committed to change. Becoming an apostolic church means renovation. It means moving forward into new things. It means we need to be not only open to but also pursuing transition and change. As one preacher so poignantly put it, "Churches will either go forward or fossilize. A fossil is an animal that didn't change during times of transition."

As with Josiah, we have not been this way before. Yet what Josiah discovered, we have access to as well, for God's Word is our blueprint from which to build. When Josiah rediscovered "the Book," it changed his life. It caused him to reevaluate the traditions of the day and go back to the patterns and purposes of God. He reached back to the biblical pattern in God's Word and God's pattern of worship, and true reformation took place throughout his realm. His story can serve to give us certain keys to reformation as we are, in this day, coming into times of apostolic reformation according to God's predestined purposes.

The first key to reformation was a return to seeking God. Josiah was a seeker; he discovered that the rewards go to the diligent seekers.

> *For in the eighth year of his reign, while he was still young, he began to seek the God of his father David; and in the twelfth year he began to purge Judah and Jerusalem of the high places, the wooden images, the carved images, and the molded images* (2 Chronicles 34:3).

We know that David was an avid seeker of God. We have many samples from the Psalms showing his heart, such as:

> *O God, You are my God; early will I seek You; my soul thirsts for You; my flesh longs for You in a dry and thirsty land where there is no water. So I have looked for You in the sanctuary, to see Your power and Your glory* (Psalm 63:1-2).

And Hebrews 11:6 states,

> *...for he who comes to God must believe that He is, and that He is a rewarder of those who diligently seek Him.*

A second key to reformation was that Josiah returned to "the Book."

> *...Hilkiah the priest found the Book of the Law of the Lord given by Moses. Then Hilkiah answered and said to Shaphan the scribe, "I*

have found the Book of the Law in the house of the Lord." And Hilki-
ah gave the book to Shaphan. So Shaphan carried the book to the
king...And Shaphan read it before the king. Thus it happened, when
the king heard the words of the Law, that he tore his clothes
(2 Chronicles 34:14-19).

Josiah took the words of "the Book" to heart. A return to "the
Book" is always a part of reform. It happened as well in the days of Ezra
and Nehemiah's reform:

And Ezra opened the book in the sight of all the people, for he was
standing above all the people; and when he opened it, all the people
stood up. And Ezra blessed the Lord, the great God. Then all the peo-
ple answered, "Amen, Amen!" while lifting up their hands. And they
bowed their heads and worshiped the Lord with their faces to the
ground. Also Jeshua, Bani, Sherebiah, Jamin, Akkub, Shabbethai,
Hodijah, Maaseiah, Kelita, Azariah, Jozabad, Hanan, Pelaiah, and
the Levites, helped the people to understand the Law; and the people
stood in their place. So they read distinctly from the book, in the Law
of God; and they gave the sense, and helped them to understand the
reading. And Nehemiah, who was the governor, Ezra the priest and
scribe, and the Levites who taught the people said to all the people,
"This day is holy to the Lord your God; do not mourn nor weep." For
all the people wept, when they heard the words of the Law. Then he
said to them, "Go your way, eat the fat, drink the sweet, and send por-
tions to those for whom nothing is prepared; for this day is holy to our
Lord. Do not sorrow, for the joy of the Lord is your strength"
(Nehemiah 8:5-10).

A third key was that Josiah was not passive about compromise and, in fact,
declared war against it.

For in the eighth year of his reign, while he was still young, he began
to seek the God of his father David; and in the twelfth year he began
to purge Judah and Jerusalem of the high places, the wooden images,
the carved images, and the molded images. They broke down the
altars of the Baals in his presence, and the incense altars which were
above them he cut down; and the wooden images, the carved images,
and the molded images he broke in pieces, and made dust of them and
scattered it on the graves of those who had sacrificed to them. He also
burned the bones of the priests on their altars, and cleansed Judah
and Jerusalem. And so he did in the cities of Manasseh, Ephraim,
and Simeon, as far as Naphtali and all around, with axes (2 Chronicles 34:3-6).

A return to God always includes a turn away from sin.

A fourth key to Josiah's success was that he was not disillusioned by the state of disrepair of the house of the Lord; rather, he gave himself to the repair of it.

> *In the eighteenth year of his reign, when he had purged the land and the temple, he sent Shaphan the son of Azaliah, Maaseiah the governor of the city, and Joah the son of Joahaz the recorder, to repair the house of the Lord his God. ... Then they put it in the hand of the foremen who had the oversight of the house of the Lord; and they gave it to the workmen who worked in the house of the Lord, to repair and restore the house* (2 Chronicles 34:8,10).

Note that he was willing to build a team ministry—to entrust the work to faithful others who shared the vision of the work.

A fifth key was that Josiah understood the prophetic significance and purpose of worship.

> *And the men did the work faithfully. Their overseers were Jahath and Obadiah the Levites, of the sons of Merari, and Zechariah and Meshullam, of the sons of the Kohathites, to supervise. Others of the Levites, all of whom were skillful with instruments of music, were over the burden bearers and were overseers of all who did work in any kind of service. And some of the Levites were scribes, officers, and gatekeepers* (2 Chronicles 34:12-13).

> *And the singers, the sons of Asaph, were in their places, according to the command of David, Asaph, Heman, and Jeduthun the king's seer...* (2 Chronicles 35:15).

In every restoration movement, music was of great importance. In David's day, we see the initial pattern for the last-days restoration of apostolic authority (tabernacle of David). David made a radical departure from Moses' form of worship and established 24-hour worship around the presence of God. From that time on, whenever there was reformation, it always included restoration of the Davidic pattern of prophetic praise, worship, and warfare. In Nehemiah's day, the completion of the walls and the implementation of the new society was inaugurated with two massive choirs so large that they circled the city and could be heard from afar (see Neh. 12).

The same return to the Davidic pattern was characteristic of Ezra's reform:

> *When the builders laid the foundation of the temple of the Lord, the priests stood in their apparel with trumpets, and the Levites, the sons*

of Asaph, with cymbals, to praise the Lord, according to the ordinance of David king of Israel. And they sang responsively, praising and giving thanks to the Lord: "For He is good, for His mercy endures forever toward Israel." Then all the people shouted with a great shout, when they praised the Lord, because the foundation of the house of the Lord was laid (Ezra 3:10-11; see also Nehemiah 12:31-36,45-46).

A sixth key was that Josiah led by example and called for commitment.

Then the king sent and gathered all the elders of Judah and Jerusalem. The king went up to the house of the Lord, with all the men of Judah and the inhabitants of Jerusalem–the priests and the Levites, and all the people, great and small. And he read in their hearing all the words of the Book of the Covenant which had been found in the house of the Lord. Then the king stood in his place and made a covenant before the Lord, to follow the Lord, and to keep His commandments and His testimonies and His statutes with all his heart and all his soul, to perform the words of the covenant that were written in this book. And he made all who were present in Jerusalem and Benjamin take a stand. So the inhabitants of Jerusalem did according to the covenant of God, the God of their fathers. Thus Josiah removed all the abominations from all the country that belonged to the children of Israel, and made all who were present in Israel diligently serve the Lord their God. All his days they did not depart from following the Lord God of their fathers (2 Chronicles 34:29-33).

Josiah led the people into a major reformation during his reign. He reestablished the rule of God through his righteous rule. Therefore, he serves today as a model of an apostolic reformer. Yet all of this was known by God from eternity past. God planned it, and it came to pass. It was prophesied, and over 300 years later, a young man came onto the scene to bring major change among the people of God. His story can serve to give us confidence as we approach these times of apostolic reformation according to God's end-time prophetic purposes.

God has declared that He will have a glorious end-time church. God will have a latter house that will be more glorious than the former. God will cause His glory to cover the earth as the waters cover the sea. God will raise up the fallen tabernacle of David and cause the ends of the earth to come to the glory of its rising. (See Isaiah 11:9; 60:1-5; Haggai 2:6-9; Habakkuk 2:14; Matthew 16:18; Acts 15:15-18.)

Great boldness, faith, and optimism will arise in our hearts when we realize that we have inherited a prophetic mission in accordance with God's inexorable purposes.

God's plan is to have a fully functioning apostolic/prophetic church in order to execute an unprecedented harvest at the end of the age...*and we're it*! We are His plan. We cannot expect the angels to do it. We cannot expect another generation to do it. God has appointed you and me to be here, now, for such a time as this.

Chapter 15

His Glorious Church

Introduction

Jesus stated that He would build His church and that even the gates of hell could not prevail against it (see Mt. 16:18). Paul the apostle stated that his ministry was one of a wise master builder who was carefully laying proper foundations within the Lord's church (see 1 Cor. 3:10-11).

The Scriptures leave no uncertainty as to what those foundations should be and what characteristics the church should display in these last days as we see the church maturing at the end of the age in all her restoration glory. Below are seven important characteristics that Jesus is building into His church and should be the goal and purpose for any local expression of His church.

Each body of believers is called to be...
- A house of prayer
- A house of praise and worship
- A supernatural church
- An evangelistic church
- An equipping church
- A sending church
- A related church

This chapter is adapted from a booklet that was originally written to clarify, in brief, the vision of our local church and to share what we believe ought to be seven characteristics of every fully functioning apostolic/prophetic church at the end of the age.

Part 1—A House of Prayer

Jesus said, "My house shall be a house of prayer" (Lk. 19:46 NAS). How essential it is that we first of all be a praying church. Second Chronicles 7:14 states, "If My people who are called by My name will humble themselves, and pray and seek My face, and turn from their wicked ways, then I will hear from heaven, and will forgive their sin and heal their land."

The fact is that things happen when we pray that don't happen when we don't pray! God's will either comes about through prayer or is thwarted by our lack of it. That is why Jesus exhorts us to pray, "Father, Thy kingdom come, Thy will be done on earth..." (see Mt. 6:9-10).

Prayer fuels the fire of God's manifested glory in the church. John Wesley stated, "God will do nothing but in answer to prayer." Charles Finney's famous statement about revival was that revival in the church was no more a mystery than that of a farmer planting a cornfield. When the farmer planted corn, he knew that he would reap a harvest of corn. When we sow sincere prayer, revival is sure to follow.

It is through prayer that we experience divine intervention into human affairs. It is by believing prayer that mountains are moved, sinners are saved, the sick are healed, and revival fires are rekindled. It is also by prayer that the human heart is transformed. Prayer is a must if we want to move beyond the realm of human strength and initiative into the realm of the supernatural power and blessing of God. If we desire the church to be all that God intended it to be, it must first of all be a praying church.

Part 2—A House of Praise and Worship

Jesus said the Father is seeking worshipers who will worship Him in spirit and truth (see Jn. 4:23-24). A very important part of our corporate life together is our worship experience, yet most Christians do not realize that the Scripture has plenty to say about how to worship.

When Moses was receiving instruction as to how he should build a place of worship before the presence of God, he was told to carefully build according to the pattern:

> *And let them construct a sanctuary for Me, that I may dwell among them. According to all that I am going to show you, as the pattern of the tabernacle and the pattern of all its furniture, just so you shall construct it. ... And there I will meet with you; and from above the mercy seat, from between the two cherubim which are upon the ark of the testimony, I will speak to you about all that I will give you in commandment for the sons of Israel* (Exodus 25:8-9,22 NAS).

We know from Hebrews 9:8-9 that the tabernacle of Moses was a symbol for this present time. However, the apostle James' statement in Acts 15:16 indicates that God is intent on restoring, through the church, the fallen tabernacle of David whose manner of worship is clearly explained in the Psalms. Even 500 years after King David, the manner of worship before God's presence was patterned after David's tabernacle (see Ezra 3:10-11). The Psalms were David's instruction manual for worship. There is a clear scriptural pattern for worship as depicted in the Psalms, as well as a clear scriptural purpose for worship.

Effective praise and worship accomplishes numerous things. The first result is the drawing of humanity to God. Psalm 100:2-4 states, "...come before His presence with singing....Enter into His gates with thanksgiving, and into His courts with praise." Scripture also states that the Lord dwells upon or inhabits the praises of His people (see Ps. 22:3 KJV).

Praise and worship transform us (see 2 Cor. 3:18). There is a cleansing and refreshing that we experience as we behold God through a sustained focus upon Him. It is during those times of unrestrained worship of Him that the loving searchlight of His Spirit probes the depths of our being, gently calling to death those things within us that would only cause us pain.

> Search me, O God, and know my heart; try me, and know my anxieties; and see if there is any wicked way in me, and lead me in the way everlasting (Psalm 139:23-24).

Anointed worship transforms us on every level—body, soul, and spirit (see 1 Sam. 16:23).

Praise and worship is also associated with the release of the gifts and anointings of the Holy Spirit. Within His presence comes His power. His anointing breaks apart yokes (see Is. 10:27), and it releases His people from all manner of oppression (see Is. 61:3). There is even a dimension of spiritual warfare released during times of high praises to God (see Ps. 149:6-9). Beyond all these things, *He is worthy of praise!* We are called to offer sacrifices of praise and thanksgiving unto Him. It pleases God for us to give Him glory and praise and honor, for surely He is worthy (see 1 Pet. 2:9; Heb. 13:15; Ps. 50:23; 69:30).

> Indeed it came to pass, when the trumpeters and singers were as one, to make one sound to be heard in praising and thanking the Lord, and when they lifted up their voice with the trumpets and cymbals and instruments of music, and praised the Lord, saying: "For He is good, for His mercy endures forever," that the house, the house of the

Lord, was filled with a cloud, so that the priests could not continue ministering because of the cloud; for the glory of the Lord filled the house of God (2 Chronicles 5:13-14).

Part 3—A Supernatural Church

Jesus said, "Truly, truly, I say to you, he who believes in Me, the works that I do shall he do also; and greater works than these shall he do; because I go to the Father" (Jn. 14:12 NAS). God has called the church to be a supernatural expression of His supernatural Kingdom. As a supernatural church, God has called us to minister "...in demonstration of the Spirit and of power, that your faith should not rest on the wisdom of men but on the power of God" (1 Cor. 2:4-5 NAS).

For the kingdom of God does not consist in words, but in power (1 Corinthians 4:20 NAS).

Jesus demonstrated the will of the Father when He exhibited signs and wonders, going about pardoning sin, healing the sick, casting out demons, and raising the dead (see Lk. 7:21-23). He then trained His disciples to do likewise and told them to train their disciples to do likewise (see Mt. 10:7-8; 28:18-20). If that weren't enough, He said that we would do even greater works than He did (see Mk. 16:17-18). There are even whole sections of the New Testament Epistles devoted to giving guidelines to the New Testament church on how to use supernatural gifts of the Holy Spirit (see Rom. 12; 1 Cor. 12–14).

The Kingdom of God is a supernatural Kingdom into which we were supernaturally birthed. We have been given supernatural "tools" for the restoration of individuals and for the building of His church. We are told to earnestly desire spiritual gifts (see 1 Cor. 12:31; 14:1) and that we are to employ our gifts "in serving one another, as good stewards of the manifold grace of God" (1 Pet. 4:10 NAS).

God has called the church to more than just religious rote and ritual and for us to be more than simply a "Christian" social club. In Second Timothy 3:1-5, we are warned that in the last days men will hold to a form of godliness but deny its power. God has called us into splendid demonstrations of love and power as He builds His church and confirms His Word with signs following (see Mk. 16:20).

Part 4—An Evangelistic Church

Jesus said, "Follow Me, and I will make you become fishers of men" (Mk. 1:17). God has entrusted us with a stewardship, for He has given us the gospel of our salvation. Jesus desires His church to be involved in outreach to the lost. This responsibility involves several things. Jesus said, "Let your light shine before men in such a way that they may see your good works, and glorify your Father who is in heaven" (Mt. 5:16 NAS). Consequently, one important aspect of evangelism is to display good works and thus demonstrate God to people. Put more simply, integrity and proper behavior before the community is an important method of evangelism.

Along with integrity and proper behavior as an evangelistic "tool," we need to couple our good deeds with a proclamation of the "good news."

How then shall they call on Him in whom they have not believed? And how shall they believe in Him of whom they have not heard? And how shall they hear without a preacher? (Romans 10:14)

And my message and my preaching were not in persuasive words of wisdom, but in demonstration of the Spirit and of power, that your faith should not rest on the wisdom of men, but on the power of God (1 Corinthians 2:4-5 NAS).

If we have experienced the mercy and grace of God; if we've tasted of the joy of sins forgiven and hope of a home in Heaven; if we've been saved, healed, delivered, and blessed; then surely we ought to share the good news with others we come in contact with. We need to get the word out through good deeds, proclamation, and demonstrations of the supernatural power of God to a lost and dying world around us. The responsibility of the church, however, goes beyond simply leading people into an initial salvation experience. Our responsibility is to assist in bringing individuals into the fullness of God's purpose for their lives.

The Sevenfold Purpose of God for Every Individual

Purpose #1: First, it is God's will that we be saved.

The Lord...is patient toward you, not wishing for any to perish but for all to come to repentance (2 Peter 3:9 NAS).

Purpose #2: God wants us delivered from every oppression and influence of the enemy.

And they may come to their senses and escape from the snare of the devil, having been held captive by him to do his will (2 Timothy 2:26 NAS).

Purpose #3: God wants us healed.

Some do not realize that it is God's will for us, but He purchased our healing on the cross and desires that we prosper and be in health even as our soul prospers (see Is. 53:4; 3 Jn. 2).

Purpose #4: God desires our sanctification.

This means God desires that we be holy, even as He is holy (see Mt. 5:48). That means we are to be separated in thought, word, and deed from that which is unclean (see 1 Thess. 4:3; Phil. 4:8).

Purpose #5: God wants us equipped.

God has called every person to be equipped for ministry and has given to the church apostles, prophets, evangelists, pastors, and teachers to do the equipping (see Eph. 4:11-16). More will be said about this in the next section of this chapter.

Purpose #6: God wants us to be activated in our sphere of service.

After having received so many things from the hand of God and His church, God wants each of us to activate our particular gifts and abilities to the furtherance of His Kingdom (see 1 Pet. 4:10).

Purpose #7: God wants us to be reproducing.

The mark of true maturity is that we can reproduce what we are in others (2 Tim. 2:2). Although at first, most of us are not able to be fully contributing members, we are not complete until we are giving forth of what we've received.

Part 5—An Equipping Church

In Ephesians 4:11-12 (NAS), Paul the apostle states that the officials of the church are to be equippers of the saints—"...for the work of service, to the building up of the Body of Christ." Unfortunately, much of the church of today has had a perspective that only the paid church staff are "ministers" and that for the rest, ministry is a spectator sport. Another problem that can often occur is that insecure leaders have been unwilling to "share" ministry lest they appear to be less needed or unimportant.

As an equipping church, we believe that every member is a potential minister. To be a minister means simply to serve with your giftings and abilities. Thus, one of our goals as a church is to teach, train, activate, and employ every member in service unto the Lord. The Scripture states in First Corinthians 12:31 and 14:1 that every saint ought to earnestly pursue spiritual giftings out of a motivation of love. Ministries can be sought, and giftings and abilities can be imparted and cultivated through training and practice.

> *And the things which you have heard from me in the presence of many witnesses, these entrust to faithful men, who will be able to teach others also* (2 Timothy 2:2 NAS; see also Hebrews 5:14).

Part 6—A Sending Church

In Romans 10:14-15, Paul the apostle states,

How then shall they call on Him in whom they have not believed? And how shall they believe in Him of whom they have not heard? And how shall they hear without a preacher? And how shall they preach unless they are sent? As it is written: "How beautiful are the feet of those who preach the gospel of peace, who bring glad tidings of good things!"

To be a sending church, we must see the larger picture of the church beyond the "local church." Put another way, we must be "apostolic." The word *apostle* means first of all to be sent, or "a sent one," though the function itself has much deeper implications. Part of being an apostolic church is to be a sending church.

There comes a time in the life of any church, just as it is with us as individuals, that unless we start giving and sharing out of what we have, we will stagnate and cease to grow. We believe we are supposed to be a contributing part of the larger body of Christ.

One of the important principles we need to understand and operate in, regarding the giving of our resources to other endeavors beyond ourselves, is the principle of sowing and reaping. Every farmer knows that you must sow the seed into the ground in order to receive a harvest, and that having sown into good soil, you can expect a greater increase from the seed sown. Although this has been a well-known teaching in the body of Christ in relation to individual and personal financial stewardship, it is a universal principle, for we see that the Scripture states, "...whatever a man sows, that he will also reap" (Gal. 6:7).

A mature church should be mindful to sow into valid, proven ministries apart from ourselves. We must be willing to send and be sent for the sake of the gospel. As a sending church, we must be willing to share—to give and to contribute people, resources, and prayer toward the furtherance of the Kingdom of God beyond ourselves and our local church. And as we are faithful to sow, God will continue to be faithful to ensure that we see a return on our seed sown in harvest.

Part 7—A Related Church

In Ephesians 2:19-21, Paul the apostle states that we are no longer alienated, but rather we are fellow citizens with the saints. We are being "fitted together" and "built together" into a dwelling of God. To be a "related" church simply means that we are connected by relationship with one another.

God insists that we be rightly related to one another. The Scriptures in First John 2:9-11; 4:19-21 imply that if we want to stay in right relationship with God, we must be about the work of maintaining a right relationship with our brothers and sisters in Christ. This means the task of building and maintaining right relationships is not an optional sideline but rather an essential ingredient of our Christian life.

Independence and isolation are sure signs of unhealthiness or immaturity. Proverbs 18:1 (NAS) states, "He who separates himself seeks his own desire, he quarrels against all sound wisdom." Instead we are to "...grow up in all aspects into Him, who is the head, even Christ, from whom the whole body, being fitted and held together by that which every joint supplies, according to the proper working of each individual part, causes the growth of the body for the building up of itself in love" (Eph. 4:15-16 NAS).

God is so concerned that we be rightly related to one another that He has inextricably connected His dealings with us to our dealings with one another. For instance, if we don't forgive others, He will not forgive us (see Mk. 11:25-26). The entire law and prophets are summarized in Matthew 22:37-40 as our being rightly related to God and to one another.

Being rightly related speaks as well to the issue of proper structure and government within the church. Being rightly fitted and held together includes understanding how to relate to spiritual authority and how to properly exercise spiritual authority.

Being a related church, however, means more than experiencing healthy relationships and proper structure within; it also means having proper relationship with the greater body of Christ. Every local church must always recognize the need to network with the larger body of Christ. Psalm 133 states that where the brethren dwell together in unity, there the Lord commands a blessing. We must always recognize that we are only a part of God's work in our city.

Proper relationship with the larger body of Christ means recognizing peer relationships as well as mentor relationships. Peer relationships with other ministries are those with whom we form alliances and coalitions for more effective ministry. We must determine to build bridges with other local ministries within our area and within our common sphere. Mentor relationships are those from whom we receive instruction, oversight, and accountability. These relationships are vital to the ongoing health of any church or ministry.

Since Scripture states that the church is built on the foundation of apostles and prophets (see Eph. 2:20), and since these ministries are more often translocal in nature rather than within the local church, we are wise to recognize their value and place in relation to the local church.

One of the vital issues of the last-days church is destined to be how to properly relate to translocal government within the body of Christ. When we see the church built together the way He intends for it to be built, it will surely be *a glorious house.*

Supplemental Readings

Bickle, Mike. *Growing in the Prophetic*. Lake Mary, FL: Creation House, 1995.

Cannistraci, Dr. David. *Apostles and the Emerging Apostolic Movement* (formerly *The Gift of Apostle*). Ventura, CA: Regal Books, 1996.

Eberle, Harold. *The Complete Wineskin* (fourth edition). Yakima, WA: WinePress Publishing, 1993.

Eckhart, John. *Moving in the Apostolic*. Ventura, CA: Renew Books, 1999.

Hamon, Dr. Bill. *Apostles, Prophets and the Coming Moves of God*. Shippensburg, PA: Destiny Image Publishers, 1997.

Hamon, Dr. Bill. *The Eternal Church*. Santa Rosa Beach, FL: Christian International Ministries Network, 1981.

Hamon, Dr. Bill. *Prophets and Personal Prophecy*. Shippensburg, PA: Destiny Image Publishers, 1987.

Hamon, Dr. Bill. *Prophets and the Prophetic Movement*. Shippensburg, PA: Destiny Image Publishers, 1990.

Hamon, Dr. Bill. *Prophets, Pitfalls and Principles*. Shippensburg, PA: Destiny Image Publishers, 1991.

Sapp, Dr. Roger. *The Last Apostles on Earth*. Shippensburg, PA: Companion Press, 1995.

Wagner, Dr. C. Peter. *Churchquake!* Ventura, CA: Regal Books, 1999.

Wagner, Dr. C. Peter. *The New Apostolic Churches*. Ventura, CA: Regal Books, 1998.

Other
*Destiny Image **titles***
you will enjoy reading

CORPORATE ANOINTING
by Kelley Varner.
Just as a united front is more powerful in battle, so is the anointing when Christians come together in unity! In this classic book, senior pastor Kelley Varner of Praise Tabernacle in Richlands, North Carolina, presents a powerful teaching and revelation that will change your life! Learn how God longs to reveal the fullness of Christ in the fullness of His Body in power and glory.
ISBN 0-7684-2011-3

A HEART FOR GOD
by Charles P. Schmitt.
This powerful book will send you on a 31-day journey with David from brokenness to wholeness. Few men come to God with as many millstones around their necks as David did. Nevertheless, David pressed beyond adversity, sin, and failure into the very forgiveness and deliverance of God. The life of David will bring hope to those bound by generational curses, those born in sin, and those raised in shame. David's life will inspire faith in the hearts of the dysfunctional, the failure-ridden, and the fallen!
ISBN 1-56043-157-1

POWER, HOLINESS, AND EVANGELISM
Contributing Authors: *Gordon Fee, Steve Beard, Dr. Michael Brown, Pablo Bottari, Pablo Deiros, Chris Heuertz, Scott McDermott, Carlos Mraida, Mark Nysewander, Stephen Seamands, Harvey Brown Jr.*
Compiled by *Randy Clark. Randy is also the author of "God Can Use Little Ole Me."*
Many churches today stress holiness but lack power, while others display great power but are deficient in personal holiness and Christian character. If we really want to win our world for Christ, we must bring both holiness and power back into our lives. A church on fire will draw countless thousands to her light. "Caution: The fire in this book may leap off the pages on to the reader. God's fire empowers, purifies, and emboldens our witness. This is the way the Church is supposed to be. Highly recommended."
—Dr. Bill Bright, Founder and President
Campus Crusade for Christ International
"The future of the Church is at stake and this book has some answers."
—Tommy Tenney, Author of *The God Chasers*
ISBN 1-56043-345-0

WHERE IS THE BODY?
by Victor Schlatter.
As a born-again Christian, you have a glorious heritage in Abraham, Isaac, and Jacob. The Bible constantly teaches concerning the power of the Jew and Gentile family of God. Victor Schlatter, a passionate church planter and Bible translator in the Australasia area, will open your eyes to the scriptural reality that there always has been and always will be one family of Abraham. He shows how the Church will not be ready as the Bride of Christ until all Jewish components of the covenant promises are fulfilled. Only then will all things close at the end of the ages as the Bible decrees!
ISBN 1-56043-339-6

Available at your local Christian bookstore.

Internet: http://www.reapernet.com

B6:93

Other
*Destiny Image **titles***
you will enjoy reading

WOMEN ON THE FRONT LINES
by Michal Ann Goll.
History is filled with ordinary women who have changed the course of their generation. Here Michal Ann Goll, co-founder of Ministry to the Nations with her husband Jim, shares how her own life was transformed and highlights nine women whose lives will impact yours! Every generation faces the same choices and issues; learn how you, too, can heed the call to courage and impact a generation.
ISBN 0-7684-2020-2

THE ASCENDED LIFE
by Bernita J. Conway.
A believer does not need to wait until Heaven to experience an intimate relationship with the Lord. When you are born again, your life becomes His, and He pours His life into yours. Here Bernita Conway explains from personal study and experience the truth of "abiding in the Vine," the Lord Jesus Christ. When you grasp this understanding and begin to walk in it, it will change your whole life and relationship with your heavenly Father!
ISBN 1-56043-337-X

THE HIDDEN POWER OF PRAYER AND FASTING
by Mahesh Chavda.
The praying believer is the confident believer. But the fasting believer is the overcoming believer. This is the believer who changes the circumstances and the world around him. He is the one who experiences the supernatural power of the risen Lord in his everyday life. An international evangelist and the senior pastor of All Nations Church in Charlotte, North Carolina, Mahesh Chavda has seen firsthand the power of God released through a lifestyle of prayer and fasting. Here he shares from decades of personal experience and scriptural study principles and practical tips about fasting and praying. This book will inspire you to tap into God's power and change your life, your city, and your nation!
ISBN 0-7684-2017-2

THE LOST ART OF INTERCESSION
by Jim Goll.
Finally there is something that really explains what is happening to so many folk in the Body of Christ. What does it mean to carry the burden of the Lord? Where is it in Scripture and in history? Why do I feel as though God is groaning within me? No, you are not crazy; God is restoring genuine intercessory prayer in the hearts of those who are open to respond to His burden and His passion.
ISBN 1-56043-697-2

Available at your local Christian bookstore.

Internet: http://www.reapernet.com

Other
Destiny Image **titles**
you will enjoy reading

Other
Destiny Image **titles**
you will enjoy reading

FAITH WORKS
by R. Russell Bixler.
The story of Russ and Norma Bixler's pioneering work in Christian television for Pittsburgh is a testimony to the power of faith in God! From a tiny trailer on a hilltop to a massive earth station and satellite uplink, Cornerstone TeleVision has touched multitudes of lives with the good news and healing power of Jesus Christ. This book will encourage you to pursue God's call on your life no matter what obstacle you face!
ISBN 1-56043-338-8

THIS GOSPEL OF THE KINGDOM
by Bertram Gaines.
What is your definition of the Kingdom of God? Some think that it's Heaven. Some think that it won't come until Jesus does. But Jesus said the Kingdom of God would come with power before all His disciples passed away! Here Bertram Gaines, teacher of the Kingdom Life Bible Seminars and a pastor, explains that the Kingdom of God is a spiritual system of righteous government. It's available to believers today, and God wants you to have a part in it!
ISBN 1-56043-323-X

FIRE IN THE WAX MUSEUM
by Hugh "Bud" Williams.
Is your church cold and frozen in tradition and religion or on fire and flowing with the power of the Holy Spirit? Today, like fire in a wax museum, the Holy Spirit is melting old forms and remolding the Church into a vessel fit for the challenges that lie before her. This awe-inspiring story tells how the Holy Spirit caught a denominational church and its pastor by surprise—and launched an international ministry out of it! Rev. Hugh "Bud" Williams, an Episcopal priest and now international minister, tells of both the joy and the pain of being in the fires of revival. *Fire in the Wax Museum* will cause you to examine the role of tradition and religion—and make you hungry for a closer and more intimate walk with the Lord.
ISBN 1-56043-344-2

THE COSTLY ANOINTING
by Lori Wilke.
In this book, teacher and prophetic songwriter Lori Wilke boldly reveals God's requirements for being entrusted with an awesome power and authority. She speaks directly from God's heart to your heart concerning the most costly anointing. This is a word that will change your life!
ISBN 1-56043-051-6

Available at your local Christian bookstore.
Internet: http://www.reapernet.com